MUCH MORE THAN
BEANS
AND
CORNBREAD

MUCH MORE THAN
BEANS
AND
CORNBREAD

Volume 2 of the Best Selling
West Virginia Cookbook

Barbara Beury McCallum

Charleston, West Virginia

Quarrier Press
Charleston, WV

cover design: Jason Queen
book design : Jason Queen/Megan Knight

ISBN 10: 1-942294-00-X
ISBN 13: 978-1-942294-00-9

Library of Congress Control Number: 2015931565

10 9 8 7 6 5 4 3 2 1

Printed in the United States of America

Distributed by:

West Virginia Book Co.
1125 Central Ave.
Charleston, WV 25302
www.wvbookco.com

CONTENTS

INTRODUCTION

"I've come a long way, baby!" to paraphrase an old cigarette commercial (Are any of you reading this old enough to remember tobacco ads?). In 1983 Mountain State Press published my first cookbook, *Mom & Ramps, Forever* which was updated and reprinted by Quarrier Press in 2010 as *Reekin' Ramp Recipes.* In 1993 *More Than Beans & Cornbread* made its debut, and twenty years later is still selling copies. First of all, I want to thank all of you who have purchased these books, and particularly those of you who have let me knew how much you enjoyed the recipes.

When my publisher, Bill Clements, approached me several years ago about doing another cookbook, I was reluctant. Not that I didn't have enough new recipes, but because it would be so different from my first two books, which are strictly West Virginia oriented. Then I thought, "Why, not?" Most people who love to cook also love to try new recipes. With our culinary horizons expanding due to the many television food programs, the Internet, and more local ethnic restaurant choices, even "died-in-the-wool" Mountaineers today enjoy more than a bowl of beans with cornbread. Also, once-hard-to-find ingredients now are readily available in our supermarkets. Years ago I had to go to an Asian market to buy my first pine nuts and ordered shallots from an ad in *Gourmet* magazine.

So here it is. The recipes are still basically uncomplicated, and I've converted many of them to take advantage of "store bought" ingredients, which certainly saves time in this busy world, and doesn't seem to drastically affect the overall taste.

BUT, here are a few of my personal idiosyncrasies when I am cooking, that if changed, could alter the taste of the original recipe.

1) I always use unsalted sweet butter, never margarine.

2) I always use freshly ground pepper and regular salt, except in soups, stews, pasta water when I use sea or Kosher salt.

3) I am not above using jarred chopped or minced garlic in a recipe if fresh isn't a necessity.

4) I'm a fan of Hellmann's Mayonnaise unless otherwise specified.

5) I always use canned low-sodium chicken or beef stock (I gave up making my own and freezing in ice cube trays years ago).

6) When in a hurry (or feeling lazy I sometimes use packaged grated Parmesan cheese from the dairy case (although the "real thing" is preferable).

7) Now, hold onto your hats! I DO NOT OWN A MICRO-WAVE OVEN, so I don't know how to use one for cooking, reheating, thawing, etc. I use a steamer for veggies and rice, and reheat all my food in a double boiler (if you don't know what this is, ask your mother or grandmother).

As another old lady cook would say, if she were still alive, BON APPETIT!

~Barbara Beury McCallum

SOUPS
& STEWS

BEEF STEW

- 1 to 1 ½ pounds Black Angus (or good quality) stew meat
- 2 medium potatoes, diced
- 1 large onion, diced
- 1 (32-ounces) container of beef stock
- 1 pound package frozen mixed vegetables (corn, carrots, peas, green beans), thawed
- salt, pepper, garlic powder
- flour
- 3-4 tablespoons butter

Pre-heat oven to 350 degrees. Dredge meat in flour seasoned with salt, pepper and garlic powder. Melt butter in ovenproof stockpot and brown meat. Add beef stock, potatoes and onion. Place covered stockpot in oven and bake for about 1 ½ hours or until meat is tender and vegetables soft. Add thawed vegetables and bake until tender (about 20-30 minutes). 4-6 servings

COLD CUCUMBER SOUP

- 6 cups chopped cucumber with skin (if waxed, cucumber must be peeled)
- 1 cup chopped onion
- 6 cups chicken broth
- 1 cup heavy cream
- 5 tablespoons finely chopped dill
- salt and pepper to taste
- 1 cup half-and-half

Simmer 4 cups chopped cucumber and onion in chicken broth until tender; about 25 minutes. Remove from heat and cool. Put cooled cucumber mixture in a blender with half-and-half, heavy cream, chopped dill, salt and pepper and blend until liquefied. Pour into a large bowl and add remaining 2 cups of chopped cucumber. Chill. Garnish with fresh dill before serving. 4-6 servings

CREAM OF ASPARAGUS SOUP

- 2 (10-ounce) packages frozen asparagus spears
- 1 cup water
- ¼ cup chopped onion
- 2 tablespoons butter
- 2 tablespoons all-purpose flour
- 1 cup milk
- 1 cup half-and-half
- ½ teaspoon salt
- dash of white pepper
- croutons (optional)

Combine first three ingredients in a saucepan; bring to boil. Separate asparagus with a fork; cover, reduce heat and simmer 5 minutes or until tender. Drain well. Place asparagus in blender and process until smooth. Melt butter in a heavy saucepan over low heat, add flour, stirring until smooth. Cook 1 minute, stirring constantly. Gradually add milk and half-and-half; cook over medium heat, stirring constantly, until mixture is thickened and bubbly. Stir in asparagus puree, salt and pepper; cook until thoroughly heated. Serve cold or hot. Garnish with croutons, if desired. Makes 4 cups

CORN CHOWDER

- 2 tablespoons butter
- 1 large onion, chopped
- 4 large potatoes, peeled and diced
- 2 ½ cups water
- l teaspoon salt
- dash of pepper
- 1 (12-ounce) can evaporated milk
- 1 (14 ¾-ounce) can cream-style corn
- 4 frankfurters, sliced into circles (optional)

Melt butter and sauté onion until soft. Add potatoes, water, salt and pepper and simmer until potatoes are tender. Add evaporated milk, creamed corn and frankfurters (if using) and cook until well heated. 6-8 servings

CREAM OF SPINACH SOUP

- 1 (10-ounce) package frozen spinach soufflé, thawed
- 1 (10 ½-ounce) can cream of potato soup
- 1 ½ cups milk
- ¼ cup sour cream
- 1 green onion, sliced
- 1 teaspoon fresh lemon juice
- pinch of dried thyme
- pepper

Place all ingredients in blender and blend until smooth. Transfer to a large, heavy saucepan. Bring to boil over medium-high heat, stirring frequently. Chill for several hours before serving. May also be served as a hot soup. 2-4 servings

CREAM OF ZUCCHINI SOUP

- 2 pounds young green zucchini
- 4 tablespoons butter
- 4 tablespoons finely chopped shallots
- 3 ¼ cups chicken broth
- 2 cloves garlic, finely chopped
- ½ teaspoon salt
- 1 cup heavy cream
- ¼ teaspoon curry powder
- croutons (optional)
- chives (optional)

Scrub zucchini. Do not peel. Slice thinly. In a heavy skillet, heat the butter and then add the zucchini, shallots and garlic. Cover tightly and simmer 15 minutes, being careful not to let brown. Put vegetables mixture in blender, then add remaining ingredients and blend until smooth. Serve hot with croutons or cold with chopped chives for garnish. 8 servings

4

CREAMY CARROT SOUP

- 2 tablespoons butter
- 1 medium onion, finely chopped
- 1 pound carrots, thinly sliced (about 3 cups)
- 4 small turnips, peeled and diced (about 2 cups)
- 1 large potato, peeled and diced (about 1 cup)
- 2 cups chicken broth
- ¼ teaspoon dried thyme
- ¼ to ½ teaspoon salt (less if using seasoned chicken broth)
- dash of black pepper
- pinch of nutmeg
- 1 large (12-ounce) can evaporated milk
- 1 to 1½ cups regular or low fat milk

In a large (at least 3-quart) saucepan melt butter and cook onion until tender, but not brown. Add broth, then stir in carrots, turnips, and potato. Bring to a boil, then lower heat to simmer. Cover and cook about 20 minutes or until vegetables are tender. Puree in blender. Return to saucepan and stir in thyme, salt, pepper, nutmeg and evaporated milk. Add enough regular milk for desired consistency. Cook soup over medium heat until heated through. Soup is delicious reheated but you may have to add more milk as it thickens upon standing. 6-8 servings

CUCUMBER YOGURT SOUP

- 1 cup plain yogurt
- l cup chicken stock
- 1 medium cucumber, peeled, seeded and chopped
- 1 clove garlic, crushed
- ½ teaspoon salt
- ¼ teaspoon hot pepper sauce
- Thin unpeeled cucumber and fresh chives for garnish

Puree all ingredients in blender. Cover and chill. Serve with thin cucumber slices and minced chives as garnish. 4 servings

EASY CHEESY BROCCOLI SOUP

- 2 large potatoes, peeled and diced
- 1 large onion, diced
- 32 ounces of chicken stock
- 1 (14 ½-ounce) can of chicken stock (optional)
- salt, pepper
- dried parsley flakes
- garlic powder
- 1 large head of fresh broccoli, washed, steamed and cut into bite size pieces or 1 (12-ounce) bag of frozen broccoli cuts, steamed
- 5-6 slices of American cheese
- milk (regular, skimmed or condensed)

Dice vegetables and add to chicken stock along with a dash salt, pepper, parsley flakes and garlic powder (to taste). Simmer until vegetables are tender. Meanwhile steam broccoli and add to soup mix, then shred American cheese and add, stirring until well blended. If soup is too thick add chicken stock or milk until soup is the consistency you like. 4-6 servings

EASY CHILI

- 1 pound ground chuck, browned and drained
- 1 (14.5-ounce) can diced tomatoes with onion and green pepper
- 1 (14.5-ounce) can stewed tomatoes with onion, green pepper, celery
- 2 (15-ounce) cans dark red kidney beans
- 1 (14-ounce) can beef broth
- 4 cloves of garlic, minced
- 3 tablespoons chili powder
- few sprinkles (to taste) of dried red pepper flakes and paprika

Mix all ingredients, stirring occasionally, until flavors well blended and chili is desired thickness. 6-8 servings

GAZPACHO

- ½ teaspoon minced garlic
- ¼ teaspoon salt
- 2 tablespoons olive oil
- 2 ¼ cups tomatoes, chopped (about 1 ½ pounds)
- ¼ cup minced green bell pepper, plus extra for garnish
- 1 cucumber, peeled and chopped
- ¼ cup minced onion, plus extra for garnish
- 1 cup vegetable juice, chilled
- 1 ½ tablespoon red wine vinegar
- dash cayenne pepper
- 3 tablespoons chopped fresh dill or garlic chives
- black pepper to taste

In a bowl mash garlic and salt together. Stir in olive oil to form a paste. Add the remaining ingredients. Stir to combine. Refrigerate until serving time. Serve in chilled soup bowls and garnish with additional chopped green peppers and onion. Recipe may be doubled or tripled. 2 large servings

GREEN ONION SOUP

- 12 green onions with tops, thinly sliced
- 3 medium potatoes, peeled and thinly sliced
- 4 cups chicken broth
- 1 (10 ¾-ounce) can cream of celery soup, undiluted
- ¾ cup evaporated milk
- ½ teaspoon salt
- ¼ teaspoon white pepper
- green onion strips (optional)

Combine first three ingredients in a large saucepan; cover and cook 10 minutes or until vegetables are tender. Strain well, reserving liquid in saucepan. Combine vegetables, soup and evaporated milk in blender; process until smooth. Add to reserved liquid. Stir in butter, salt and pepper. Cook over low heat, stirring often, until thoroughly heated. Serve cold or hot. Garnish with green onion strips, if desired. Makes 7 cups

HAM AND COLLARD STEW

- 1 large sweet onion, diced (about 1 ½ cup)
- 3 celery ribs, diced
- 8 ounces of ham steak, diced
- 1 teaspoon vegetable oil
- 1 (14-ounce) can fat-free chicken stock
- 1 (28-ounce) can diced tomatoes
- 1 pound package of fresh collard greens, washed, trimmed and chopped
- 3 (15 ½-ounce) cans pinto beans, rinsed and drained

Sauté diced onion, celery and ham in hot vegetable oil in a large Dutch oven over medium heat 8 minutes or until onion tender. Stir in chicken stock, diced tomatoes, and chopped collard greens; bring to a boil. Cover, reduce heat, and simmer, stirring occasionally, about 45 minutes. Stir in beans and simmer, stirring occasionally, 10 minutes, or until mixed thoroughly. 8-10 servings.

HAMBURGER SOUP

- 1 pound ground chuck
- 1 medium onion, chopped
- 1 (14 ½-ounce) can whole tomatoes, un-drained
- 1 teaspoon Worcestershire sauce
- 1 (12-ounce) package frozen mixed vegetables
- 1 cup medium egg noodles, uncooked
- 4 cups water
- 2 beef bouillon cubes
- 1 teaspoon salt
- ½ to 1 teaspoon pepper
- 1 bay leaf
- ¾ cup sliced celery
- ½ teaspoon dried whole thyme

Cook ground chuck and onion over medium heat until browned. Drain mixture and discard pan drippings. Add next 8 ingredients; bring to boil. Reduce heat, cover and simmer about 30 minutes. Add vegetables, noodles and thyme. Bring to a boil, reduce heat and simmer uncovered about 20 minutes, stirring occasionally. 6-8 servings

HEARTY NAVY BEAN SOUP

- 1 ½ cups dried navy beans
- 1 large ham hock
- 3 cloves of garlic, minced
- 4 cups water
- 2 large onions, chopped
- 2-3 large potatoes, peeled and cubed
- Turnip greens **
- 4-5 cups water (use 4 cups if 2 potatoes and 5 cups if 3 potatoes)
- 2 teaspoons salt
- ½ teaspoon pepper

**May use 16 ounces frozen turnip greens with chopped turnips (thawed) but cut back on potatoes or use 1 (14 ½-ounce) canned turnip greens (low sodium-no salt added).

Sort and wash beans, cover with 2 inches of water and soak overnight. Drain beans and add ham hock, garlic and 4 cups of water. Bring to a boil, cover, reduce heat and simmer about 1-2 hours or until beans are soft but not mushy. Add onions, potatoes, salt and pepper, cover and simmer about 1 hour (stirring occasionally) or until vegetables are tender. Add turnip greens and cook until heated. Makes about 3 quarts

LANDLUBBER'S CHOWDER

- 6 large potatoes, peeled and diced
- 4 stalks celery, diced
- 2 large onions, diced
- 2-3 carrots, peeled and diced
- 1 (15-ounce) can of corn
- 1 large (12-ounce) can tuna, drained
- 5-6 slices American cheese, torn into small pieces
- milk (evaporated or regular)
- ½ to 1 stick butter
- salt, pepper
- garlic powder

Place potatoes, celery, onions, and carrots in large pot with enough water to cover. Add salt, pepper, and a little garlic powder. Cook until tender. Stir in corn, tuna, American cheese, butter and continue stirring until cheese and butter are melted. Add milk until desired consistency (I usually start with 1 can of evaporated milk, then thin if necessary with skim milk). 8 servings

LEFT OVER TURKEY (CHICKEN) RICE SOUP

- 2 (32-ounce) containers of chicken stock
- 2 carrots, peeled and diced
- 2 stalks celery, diced
- 1 medium onion, diced
- salt and pepper
- garlic powder
- 1 tablespoon dried parsley flakes
- 1 cup rice, uncooked
- 2 cups diced left over turkey or chicken

Place vegetables in stock and add salt, pepper, garlic powder to taste plus parsley flakes. Simmer until vegetables tender. Add cup of rice, cover and bring to boil, uncover and simmer until rice done. Add turkey/chicken and heat through. Add additional chicken stock if soup is too thick and correct seasonings, if necessary. 6-8 servings

POTATO SOUP

- 8 slices bacon, minced
- 1 ½ cups diced onions
- ½ cup diced celery
- 4 pounds potatoes, pared and cubed
- 2 tablespoons instant chicken bouillon granules
- 2 ½ quarts water
- ½ teaspoon salt
- ¼ teaspoon freshly ground pepper
- 1 tablespoon fresh chopped chives, for garnish

Fry bacon in a large heavy 6-quart pot until golden brown. Remove from pot and drain. Sauté onion and celery in bacon drippings until soft; drain. Pour off all but 2 tablespoons of drippings. Add bacon, celery, onion, potatoes, bouillon granules and water. Bring to a boil, reduce heat to medium, cover and cook for about 1 ¾ hours (until potatoes tender). Add salt and pepper after removing from heat. Top with sprinkling of chives when serving. 6-8 servings

SAUSAGE BEAN SOUP

- 1 (16-ounce) package dried red kidney beans
- 6 cups water
- 2 pounds beef soup bones
- 2 teaspoon salt
- 2 (8-ounce) cans tomato sauce
- 2 medium potatoes, cubed
- 2 medium carrots, thinly sliced
- ¾ pound Polish sausage, cut into ½-inch slices
- 2 stalks celery, chopped
- 2 medium onions, chopped
- 1 small head of cabbage, coarsely chopped
- pepper to taste

Cover beans with water and soak overnight. Drain beans, add 6 cups water, soup bones and salt. Bring to a boil. Cover, reduce heat and cook about 45 minutes or until beans tender; discard soup bones. Add tomato sauce, potatoes and carrots; cover and simmer about 10 minutes. Add remaining ingredients; cover and simmer 10-15 minutes or until vegetables are tender. 6-8 servings

SHRIMP MUSHROOM SOUP

- ½ pound of cooked medium shrimp (peeled and de-veined)
- ¼ pound fresh mushrooms, sliced
- ¼ cup chopped green onions
- 1 ½ tablespoons butter, melted
- 1 (10 ¾-ounce) can cream of mushroom soup
- 1 clove garlic, minced
- 1 (10 ¾-ounce) can New England clam chowder
- 1 cup whipping cream
- 1 cup water
- dash pepper

Sauté mushrooms, onions and garlic in butter in Dutch oven about 2 minutes (until soft). Add shrimp. Combine soups, whipping cream, water and pepper; mix well. Add to shrimp mixture, stirring well. Cook until thoroughly heated. 4 servings

SIMPLE CUCUMBER SOUP

- 1 medium cucumber, peeled and diced
- 1 ¼ cups water
- 1 (10 ¾-ounce) can cream of chicken soup
- chopped fresh chives for garnish

Cover cucumber with water and cook until tender; about 10 minutes. Do not drain. Blend in soup. Chill and garnish with chives before serving. 3-4 servings

TOASTY FRENCH ONION SOUP

- 4 large (or 6 medium) onions, thinly sliced
- ¼ cup butter, melted
- 2 teaspoons flour
- 1 (32-ounce) can of beef broth
- 1 teaspoon Worcestershire sauce
- dash of pepper
- 4 slices French bread, toasted
- grated Parmesan cheese

Sauté onion in butter in a Dutch oven over medium heat until tender, stirring frequently. Add 2 teaspoons of flour and stir with onions for a few minutes. Add broth, Worcestershire, and pepper, bring to a boil. Reduce heat; cover and simmer 5 minutes. Ladle soup into individual baking bowls; top each with a slice of toasted bread. Sprinkle with cheese. Place under broiler 2-3 minutes to brown top. Serve immediately. 4 servings

TUSCANY BEAN SOUP

- 1 pound dried small white or lima beans
- 1 quart water
- 1 (32-ounces) container chicken stock
- 4 bay leaves
- 2 teaspoons dried oregano
- 6 tablespoons olive oil
- 2 teaspoons salt
- ¼ cup finely chopped fresh parsley
- 4 cloves garlic, crushed
- 5 tablespoons lemon juice

Soak beans overnight. Drain and cover with water and stock in large pot. Add bay leaves. oregano, olive oil. Bring to a boil, reduce heat, cover and simmer until beans are tender (about one hour). Add salt. Puree ½ the beans in blender/food processor with ½ the liquid and then return to pot with whole beans and remaining liquid. Add parsley, garlic and lemon juice and simmer about 10 more minutes until well heated. 4-6 servings

ENTRÉES

APPLE LUNCHEON QUICHE

- 2 unbaked prepared piecrusts
- 2 cups shredded Swiss cheese
- ½ pound sausage, cooked, crumbled and drained
- 2 cups apples, peeled and sliced
- 4 ounces of canned, sliced mushrooms
- 4 eggs
- 1 tablespoon flour
- 1 teaspoon salt
- 1 cup milk
- 1 cup evaporated milk
- 1 ½ tablespoons melted butter

Pre-heat oven to 375 degrees. In each piecrust layer half of the cheese, sausage, apples and mushrooms IN THAT ORDER. Mix eggs, flour, salt, milks and butter and pour over layered ingredients in piecrusts. Bake until firm, about 45 minutes. Let stand five minutes before serving. 6-8 servings

ASPARAGUS QUICHE

- 1 frozen piecrust, baked according to directions
- about 20 fresh asparagus
- 1 ¼ cups cream
- 3 eggs
- salt and pepper to taste
- 4 to 6 ounces grated Parmesan and Gruyere
  (or regular Swiss cheese)
- Dijon mustard

Pre-heat oven to 350 degrees. Blanch asparagus and cool. Cover bottom of piecrust with Dijon mustard and arrange asparagus in single layer. Combine cream, eggs and seasonings and pour over asparagus. Thickly cover top with mixture of grated cheeses. Bake for 30 minutes or until eggs set. 4 servings

BAKED APRICOT CHICKEN

- 4 pounds of chicken (boneless breasts are good)
- 1 package dry onion soup mix
- 4 tablespoons soy sauce
- 4 tablespoons honey
- 1 large can apricots, juice and all

Pre-heat oven to 350 degrees. Mix all sauce ingredients well. Place chicken in large baking dish in one layer. Cover with sauce and bake for 1 ½ to 2 hours. 6-8 servings

BARBEQUED SPARERIBS

- 4 pounds pork spareribs

  Sauce: melt in saucepan
- 1 stick of butter
- ¾ cup catsup
- 1 ½ cup dark brown sugar
- 3 tablespoons lemon juice
- 1 tablespoon Dijon mustard
- 2 teaspoons steak sauce
- 2 teaspoons hot pepper sauce
- 2 teaspoons Worcestershire sauce

Pre-heat oven to 350 degrees. Sprinkle ribs lightly with salt, put on a rack in a roasting pan and spread with some of the sauce. Bake for 30 minutes. Continue baking spareribs, spreading them with additional sauce every 15 minutes for one hour or until tender. 4 servings

BARBEQUED PORK OR BEEF (SANDWICH)

- 1 ½ to 2 cups shredded pork or beef roast
- 1 ½ tablespoon Worcestershire sauce
- 1 cup catsup
- 1 ½ cup brown sugar
- 1 tablespoon prepared mustard
- 1 tablespoon vinegar
- 1 tablespoon garlic powder

Simmer over low heat until you get the consistency and taste you want. Good for leftover pork or beef roast. Serve on hamburger buns with slaw (if desired). 4-6 servings

BEEF AND MUSHROOM LASAGNE

- 1 can (10 ¾ ounce) cream of mushroom soup
- ¼ cup milk
- 1 pound ground chuck
- 1 (24-ounce) jar Prego Fresh Mushroom Italian Sauce
- 9 cooked lasagne noodles
- 1 cup shredded 6-cheese Italian blend

Pre-heat oven to 400 degrees. Stir soup and milk together in a small bowl until smooth. Brown beef and drain fat. Add the jar of Italian sauce. Starting with sauce, layer with 3 noodles and 1 cup soup mixture in a shallow 2-quart baking dish long enough to hold noodles. Top with 3 more noodles, layer of Italian sauce, 3 more noodles and top with remaining soup mixture. Sprinkle with cheese to cover top of dish well. Cover baking dish with foil and bake 30 minutes or until hot and bubbly. Let stand 10 minutes before cutting. 6 servings

BEEF SPANISH RICE

- ¼ cup vegetable oil
- 1 medium onion, thinly sliced
- ½ medium green pepper, chopped
- 1 pound lean ground beef
- 1 cup regular rice, uncooked
- 2 (8-ounce) cans Hunt's tomato sauce
- 1 ¾ cup hot water
- 1 teaspoon each salt, pepper
- 1 teaspoon prepared mustard
- dash of dried oregano

Heat oil in large skillet. Add onion, green pepper, ground beef and rice. Stir until lightly browned. Add tomato sauce and remaining ingredients. Mix, bring to quick boil, cover and simmer for about 25 minutes (until rice done). 6-8 servings

BLUE PASTA PRIMAVERA

- 10 plum tomatoes
- 1 red or green bell pepper
- 1 yellow squash
- 2 green onions
- ¼ cup red wine vinegar
- ¼ cup olive oil
- 2 tablespoons Dijon mustard
- ½ teaspoon each, salt and pepper
- 1 cup sliced fresh mushrooms
- 2 tablespoons olive oil
- 8 ounces fettuccine or linguine, cooked
- 4 ounces crumbled blue cheese

Seed and chop tomatoes, Cut bell pepper and squash into thin strips. Slice green onions. Set vegetables aside. Combine vinegar and next 4 ingredients in a jar; cover and shake vigorously. Sauté bell pepper, squash, green onions and mushrooms in 2 tablespoons hot oil until crisp-tender. Stir in chopped tomato and vinegar mixture; cook over medium heat, stirring occasionally, until thoroughly heated. Toss with pasta and sprinkle with blue cheese. 4 servings

BROCCOLI PASTA AND PESTO

- 1 pound of fresh broccoli, stems removed and florets cut into large pieces
- ½ cup pine nuts
- 2 garlic cloves, chopped
- ½ cup freshly grated Parmesan cheese
- ¼ cup extra-virgin olive oil
- pasta of choice

In a large saucepan of boiling, salted water, cook broccoli until very tender (about 5-6 minutes). Reserve about ¼ cup cooking water. Drain broccoli well. In a small non-stick dry skillet cook pine nuts and garlic over moderate heat, stirring, until pale golden. In a blender or food processor blend together broccoli, pine nuts, garlic, reserved cooking water. Add Parmesan and olive oil until smooth. Serve over pasta of choice. May refrigerate leftover sauce. Makes about 2 cups

BOILED ONE POT DINNER

- 1 (12-ounce) can corned beef
- 1 (14-ounce) can beef stock
- 6 carrots, peeled and cut in one-inch slices
- 6 potatoes peeled and cut in one-inch slices
- cabbage, medium head, cut into quarters
- 1 large onion, quartered

Pour beef stock into large soup pot and add ¾ to 1 can of water. Add carrots, potatoes and onion and cook (covered) about 30-40 minutes. Uncover and add cabbage and cook another 20 minutes or until vegetables tender. In last 10 minutes of cooking time, add can of corned beef and coarsely break up into pieces. 4-6 servings

BOURBON GLAZED HAM

- 1 (10-pound) fully cooked smoked ham
- ¾ cup whole cloves
- ¾ cup bourbon or apple juice
- 2 cups dark brown sugar
- 1 tablespoon dry mustard
- 2 navel oranges, sliced

Pre-heat oven to 325 degrees. Wrap ham in aluminum foil and place in a lightly greased 13 x 9-inch roasting pan. Bake for 2 hours. Remove ham from oven, and increase temperature to 450 degrees. Unwrap ham; discard foil. Remove skin and excess fat from ham. Make ¼ inch deep cuts in a diamond design, and insert cloves at 1-inch intervals. Brush ham evenly with ¼ cup bourbon or apple juice. Stir together remaining ½ cup bourbon or apple juice, sugar and mustard in a small bowl. Pat sugar mixture evenly over ham; arrange orange slices over sugar and secure with wooden toothpicks. Lightly baste with drippings; bake 15-20 minutes or until meat thermometer inserted into thickest portion registers 140 degrees and sugar has melted and formed a glaze. Let stand 15 minutes before slicing. 15-20 servings

CHEESE BAKED FISH

- 2 tablespoons butter
- 3 tablespoons flour
- ¾ teaspoon salt
- ⅛ teaspoon nutmeg
- 2 pounds fish fillets (haddock, perch, flounder or sole)
- 1 cup hot milk
- ¾ teaspoon lemon juice
- ½ cup shredded cheddar cheese
- ½ teaspoon dry mustard

Pre-heat oven to 375 degrees. Melt butter and blend in dry ingredients. Stir in milk and cook until thickened, stirring constantly. Add lemon juice and cheese. Stir until cheese melts. Place fish in greased baking dish and cover with sauce. Bake for 40 minutes. 6 servings

21

CHICKEN AND DUMPLINGS

- 4 tablespoons solid shortening
- 4 tablespoons flour
- 2 teaspoons salt
- 1 cup milk
- 1 cup chicken stock
- 1 cup sliced mushrooms
- 2 teaspoons chopped onion
- 1 ½ to 2 cups diced cooked chicken

Melt shortening in Dutch oven and blend in flour and salt. Add milk and chicken stock. Cook over low heat until smooth and thickened, stirring often. Stir in mushrooms, onion and chicken. Blend well.

Dumplings:
- 1 cup sifted enriched flour
- 1 ½ teaspoons double-acting baking powder
- ½ teaspoon salt
- 2 tablespoons melted solid shortening
- ½ cup milk

Make dumplings by combining dry ingredients with melted shortening and milk. Blend enough to moisten. Drop from teaspoon into hot chicken mixture.

Cover tightly and cook for 15 minutes over medium heat, WITHOUT REMOVING COVER. For puffy, fluffy dumplings, don't peek while they are cooking. 4-6 servings

CHICKEN AND NOODLES

- 1 (10 ¾-ounces) can mushroom soup
- ½ cup milk
- 2 cups medium noodles, cooked and drained
- 2 cups cooked chicken, cubed (left over or prepared packaged)**
- ¼ cup grated Parmesan cheese
- ¼ teaspoon black pepper
- 1 small can mushroom stems and pieces

Pre-heat oven to 350 degrees. Stir soup and milk together. Add to noodles, chicken and mushrooms. Add Parmesan cheese and pepper and mix well. Bake about 30 minutes or until dish hot through. May add another sprinkling of Parmesan on top of noodles in last 5 minutes. 4-6 servings

** May use tuna

CHICKEN-BROCCOLI CASSEROLE

- 2 packages (12-ounces) frozen broccoli, cooked tender-crisp
- 3 large chicken breasts cooked (about 12-ounces)**
- 2 (4-ounce) cans mushrooms
- 2 (10 ¾-ounce) cans cream of mushroom soup
- 6 ounces packaged stuffing mix prepared as directed or:

Stuffing:
- 6 slices bread, cubed
- ¾ teaspoon dry onion, ¾ teaspoon salt, scant poultry seasoning mixed together and moistened with chicken broth to right consistency

** Cook 3 large chicken breasts in large pot with 2 cups water, 1 teaspoon salt until tender.

Pre-heat oven to 350 degrees. Skin and shred meat. Or use equivalent of prepared chicken. Place broccoli in casserole dish and top with chicken and mushrooms. Cover with soup. Spread top with moist stuffing. Bake uncovered for 30-45 minutes, until thoroughly heated. 8 servings

CHICKEN MANICOTTI

- 8 manicotti shells
- 1 (10 ¾-ounce) can creamy chicken mushroom soup
- ½ cup sour cream
- 2 cups chopped cooked chicken
- ¼ cup chopped onion
- 1 (4-ounce) can sliced mushrooms, drained
- 2 tablespoons butter, melted
- ¼ cup warm water
- ½ teaspoon chicken bouillon granules
- 1 cup (4-ounces) shredded cheddar cheese

Pre-heat oven to 350 degrees. Cook manicotti shells according to package directions, omitting salt; drain and set aside. Combine soup and sour cream; mix well. Combine half of soup mixture and chicken and mix well. Reserve remaining soup mixture. Stuff manicotti shells with chicken mixture; place in a greased 12 x 8 x 2-inch baking dish. Sauté onion and mushrooms in butter until tender; set aside. Combine water and bouillon granules, stirring until dissolved and add to reserved soup mixture.

Stir soup mixture into mushroom mixture and mix well. Spoon over manicotti; bake for 15 minutes. Sprinkle with cheddar cheese and bake for an additional 5 minutes. 4-6 servings

CHICKEN MIMOSA

- 6 whole boneless chicken breasts
- 2 eggs, beaten
- 1 ½ teaspoon salt
- ¼ teaspoon white pepper
- ½ cup flour
- 6 tablespoons butter
- 6 slices Prosciutto ham
- 6 slices Mozzarella cheese
- ½ cup chicken broth

Put breasts between sheets of wax paper and pound until about ¼- inch thick. Mix beaten eggs with salt and pepper. Dip breasts in egg mixture, then flour. Melt the butter in a large stick-free skillet; add chicken and brown on both sides. Place a slice of ham on each chicken breast and cover with a slice of cheese. Add the broth, cover and cook over low heat about 5 minutes. 6 servings

CHICKEN ON A BUN

- 3 large cloves of garlic, skin on
- ¼ cup mayonnaise
- 1 teaspoon finely grated lemon zest
- pepper to taste
- 2 small skinless, boneless chicken breasts
- 2 teaspoons olive oil
- 4 tablespoons fresh lemon juice
- salt and pepper, to taste
- 4 hamburger buns
- 8 leaves Boston or Bibb lettuce

Place garlic in a small saucepan. Cover with water and bring to a boil. Reduce heat. Cook for 25 minutes. Drain, slip skins off. Mash and mix with mayonnaise, lemon zest and pepper. Refrigerate garlic-mayonnaise until ready to use.

Preheat broiler. Cut chicken breasts in half lengthwise and fan out the fillet. Lay flat on a baking sheet. Brush each breast with oil, drizzle with lemon juice and sprinkle with salt and pepper. Place under broiler, 4 inches from heat, and cook for 4-5 minutes, until cooked through but moist. Open buns and lightly toast. Spread both sides of the buns with prepared garlic mayonnaise. Lay a chicken breast on bun and top with lettuce. 4 servings

CHICKEN STIR-FRY

- 3 tablespoons soy sauce
- 2 tablespoons dry sherry
- 1 tablespoon cornstarch
- 2 cloves garlic, minced
- 2 tablespoons extra-light olive oil
- 2 whole boneless chicken breasts, thinly sliced
- 1 small onion, thinly sliced
- 1 carrot, pared and thinly sliced
- ½ pound broccoli, cut into bite-size pieces

Combine soy sauce, sherry, cornstarch, garlic and ¼ cup water; set aside. In wok or large skillet, stir-fry chicken in hot oil for 2 minutes. Add vegetables; stir-fry 4 minutes. Add soy sauce mixture; cook and stir until slightly thickened. 4 servings

CHICKEN RISOTTO

- 6 tablespoons butter
- 1 pound boneless chicken breasts, cut into thin strips
- 1 clove garlic, minced
- 1 ½ cups uncooked rice
- ¼ pound mushrooms, sliced
- 3 green onions (tops optional) chopped
- 3 cups chicken broth
- 1 teaspoon basil
- 1 cup shredded cheddar cheese

In a large skillet, melt butter, add chicken and cook over medium heat, stirring constantly, until pieces are brown, about 5 minutes. Remove chicken from skillet. Add remaining butter, rice and garlic to skillet and cook, stirring constantly, until rice is lightly brown, about 5 minutes. Add mushrooms and green onion. Continue cooking, stirring occasionally, until mushrooms are tender, about 2 minutes. Stir in chicken broth and basil. Bring to a boil, cover and simmer 15 minutes. Gently stir in chicken. Continue simmering until chicken is heated through and rice is tender, about 5 minutes. Top with cheese and serve immediately. 6 servings

CHICKEN VEGETABLE STIR FRY

- 2 tablespoons cornstarch
- ¼ teaspoon ground ginger
- 1 container (14.5 ounces) vegetable broth
- 1 tablespoon soy sauce
- 3 tablespoons vegetable oil
- 1 pound skinless, boneless chicken, cut into strips
- 5 cups cut-up fresh vegetables (broccoli, mushrooms, carrots, celery, green onions)
- 1 clove garlic, minced

Stir together cornstarch, ginger, broth and soy until smooth; set aside. In large skillet in 2 tablespoons hot oil, stir-fry half of the chicken until browned. Remove; set aside and repeat with remaining chicken. Add remaining 1 tablespoon oil to skillet and in hot oil stir-fry vegetables with garlic until tender-crisp. Reduce heat to medium. Stir in reserved chicken and broth mixture. Cook until mixture boils and thickens, stirring constantly. Serve over rice.*
4 servings

*May use any left over vegetable broth instead of water while cooking rice for great taste.

CRAB AND ASPARAGUS PIE

- 4 ounces crabmeat, shredded
- 12 ounces fresh asparagus, cooked
- ½ cup chopped onion, cooked
- 1 cup shredded Monterey Jack cheese
- ¼ cup grated Parmesan cheese pepper to taste
- ¾ cup all-purpose flour
- ¾ teaspoon baking powder
- ½ teaspoon salt
- 2 tablespoons butter, chilled
- 1 ½ cups milk
- 4 eggs

Preheat oven to 350 degrees. Lightly grease a 10-inch quiche dish or pie plate. Layer crabmeat, asparagus and onion in pie plate. Top with cheeses and season with pepper. Combine flour, baking powder and salt in a large bowl. With pastry blender or 2 knives, cut in butter. Add milk and eggs; stir until blended. Pour over vegetables and cheeses. Bake about 30 minutes or until filling is puffed and knife inserted near center comes out clean. 6 servings

CRABMEAT AND PARMESAN QUICHE

- 1 refrigerator piecrust placed in 9-inch pie pan and baked as directed
- 3 or 4 green onions, chopped
- 2 teaspoons olive oil
- 12 ounces lump crabmeat, rinsed and drained
- 1 teaspoon grated lemon rind
- ½ teaspoon Old Bay seasoning
- ⅛ teaspoon ground red pepper
- 1 cup half-and-half
- 3 large eggs
- ¼ teaspoon EACH salt and pepper
- 5 ounces shredded Parmesan cheese

Pre-heat oven to 400 degrees. Sauté green onions in hot oil in a large skillet over medium-high for 2 minutes. Stir in crabmeat and next 3 ingredients; sauté about 2 minutes. Whisk together half-and-half and next 3 ingredients in a large bowl; stir in cheese and crabmeat mixture. Pour into prepared crust. Bake on lowest oven rack for 35-40 minutes or until set. Let stand 15 minutes before serving. 6 servings

CRABMEAT CASSEROLE

- 4 cups crabmeat
- 1 cup mayonnaise
- 1 tablespoon dry mustard
- 1 tablespoon Worcestershire sauce
- ½ cup slivered almonds
- ½ cup chopped celery
- salt and pepper to taste
- ¼ cup Parmesan cheese

Pre-heat oven to 375 degrees. Butter shallow baking dish. Mix all ingredients, except cheese and toss lightly. Place in the baking dish and sprinkle with the Parmesan cheese. Bake about 25 minutes. About 6 servings

CREAMY SMOKED SALMON AND PASTA

- 2 tablespoons butter
- 1 large garlic clove, finely chopped
- 1 large whole green onion, finely chopped
- 6 ounces smoked salmon, trimmed and cut into julienne strips
- ¾ cup heavy or whipping cream
- ⅛ teaspoon grated nutmeg
- ¼ teaspoon dried basil
- pepper to taste
- 1 tablespoon grated Parmesan cheese

Melt butter in a medium skillet. Add garlic and green onion and cook for 1 minute. Add salmon and sauté for 2 minutes, then stir in cream, nutmeg, basil and pepper. Cook until sauce thickens slightly. Stir in Parmesan cheese and serve over hot fettuccine (or spaghetti). 4 servings

CROCK-POT PORK CHOPS

- 6 (1-inch thick) lean pork chops
- 1 (10 ¾-ounce) can chicken broth
- 2 tablespoons vegetable oil
- ½ cup all purpose flour
- 1 ½ teaspoons dry mustard
- ½ teaspoon salt
- ½ teaspoon garlic powder

Combine flour, dry mustard, salt and garlic powder in a shallow dish, dredge chops in flour mixture and set aside. Combine remaining flour mixture and chicken broth in a 3 ½-quart crock-pot. Pour oil into a large skillet and heat until hot. Brown chops on both sides and place in crock-pot. Cook, covered on high 2- 2 ½ hours or until tender. Serve with rice or mashed potatoes. 6 servings

CROCK-POT RIBS AND KRAUT

- 2 cans (15-ounces each) Bavarian sauerkraut
- 2 pounds country style pork ribs

Place sauerkraut in bottom of crock-pot. Season pork ribs with salt and pepper and place on top or kraut. Cook on high for two hours, then on low until tender (about 5 hours). 4-6 servings

CRUSTLESS SPINACH PIE

- 12 ounces fresh baby spinach
- ¼ cup butter
- 3 tablespoons all purpose flour
- ¼ teaspoon salt
- ¼ teaspoon pepper
- ¼ teaspoon garlic powder
- 4 large eggs, lightly beaten
- ¾ cup whipping cream
- ½ cup shredded Parmesan cheese

Pre-heat oven to 350 degrees. Rinse spinach well; drain. Melt butter in a large skillet over medium heat. Add spinach, and cook until just wilted. Combine flour, salt, pepper, and garlic powder in a large bowl. Add spinach, eggs, whipping cream, and Parmesan cheese, stirring well. Pour mixture into a lightly greased 9-inch pie pan. Bake for 25 minutes or until knife inserted in middle comes out clean. Let stand 10 minutes before serving. 8 servings

EASY BAKED SHRIMP

- ¼ cup canola oil
- 1 ½ pounds peeled and de-veined shrimp
- 1 tablespoon minced garlic (may use jarred)
- ½ teaspoon salt
- ¼ teaspoon pepper
- ½ cup Italian seasoned breadcrumbs
- 3 tablespoons chopped fresh parsley
- lemon wedges (optional)

Pre-heat oven to 475 degrees. Pour canola oil into a 13 x 9 x 2-inch baking dish. Add shrimp and sprinkle with garlic, salt and pepper, and then toss with breadcrumbs and parsley. Bake for 5 minutes. Turn shrimp gently and bake 3-5 minutes more, or until shrimp are pink and breadcrumbs brown. Serve with lemon wedges and rice, if desired. This dish may be prepared a few hours before cooking and refrigerated. 4 servings

EASY MACARONI AND CHEESE

- 8 ounces of macaroni
- 1 (1-pound) jar Ragu Double Cheddar Cheese sauce
- butter
- pepper
- Italian breadcrumbs
- milk

Pre-heat oven to 350 degrees. Cook macaroni for 7 minutes and drain. While still hot, mix with butter and pepper (salt if not cooked in salted water). Stir in at least ¾ jar of Ragu cheese sauce and mix well. Pour into a greased 1 ¾ quart casserole and top with breadcrumbs. Cover with milk and bake uncovered in oven for 40-50 minutes. 4-6 servings

EASY MEAT LOAF

- 1 pound lean ground beef
- ½ cup uncooked quick-cooking oats
- 1 tablespoon instant minced onion, dried
- 1 tablespoon dried parsley flakes
- celery flakes
- 1 teaspoon salt
- ½ teaspoon pepper
- 1 tablespoon Worcestershire sauce
- 2 tablespoons catsup
- 1 large egg, beaten
- ½ cup milk
- 3 bacon slices

Pre-heat oven to 350 degrees. Combine first 11 ingredients; shape into a loaf and place in a lightly greased 13 x 9-inch pan. Top with bacon slices. Bake for 45 minutes or until done. 4 servings

EASY SHRIMP SCAMPI

- ½ cup butter, melted
- 3 cloves garlic, crushed
- 2 tablespoons olive oil
- 2 tablespoons fresh chopped parsley (I prefer Italian)
- 2 tablespoons dry white wine
- 1 tablespoon lemon juice
- 24 large or jumbo shrimp, peeled and de-veined
- salt and pepper to taste
- cooked pasta (angel hair is nice, or rice)

Heat butter, garlic and olive oil in a large skillet. Add shrimp and sauté on both sides (about 5 minutes) until done. Remove shrimp and keep warm. Pour pan drippings into a small saucepan. Add the remaining ingredients. Cook over high heat for about one minute. Pour sauce over shrimp and serve over pasta or rice. 4 servings

EGG BAKE

- 1 tablespoon vegetable oil
- 4 green onions, chopped
- 4 ounces of mushrooms, sliced
- 1 cup low-fat cottage cheese
- 1 cup sour cream
- 6 eggs
- 2 tablespoons all-purpose flour
- ¼ teaspoon salt
- ⅛ teaspoon pepper
- dash of hot pepper sauce

Pre-heat oven to 350 degrees. Crease a shallow 1-quart baking dish. Heat oil in medium skillet over medium heat and sauté onions and mushrooms until tender. Set aside. In blender or food processor, process cottage cheese until almost smooth. Add sour cream, eggs, flour, salt, pepper and hot pepper sauce; process until combined. Stir in onions and mushrooms. Pour into the greased baking dish. Bake about 40 minutes or until knife inserted near center comes out clean. 6 servings

END OF SUMMER VEGETABLE BAKE

- 1 small head cauliflower, broken into small florets (about 5 cups)
- 1 medium bunch broccoli, cut into small florets (about 4 cups)
- 1 medium onion, chopped
- 2 cloves of garlic, minced
- 1 tablespoon butter
- 2 medium tomatoes, chopped
- ¾ teaspoon dried basil
- ¾ teaspoon dried oregano
- ¾ teaspoon salt
- ¼ teaspoon pepper
- ¼ teaspoon hot pepper sauce
- 4 eggs
- ½ cup half-and-half
- 1 ½ cups (6-ounces) shredded Swiss cheese, divided
- ¼ cup shredded (fresh, if possible) Parmesan cheese

Pre-heat oven to 375 degrees. Place the cauliflower and broccoli in a saucepan with a small amount of water. Bring to a boil. Reduce heat; cover and simmer for 5 to 10 minutes or until tender-crisp. Drain and set aside. In a large skillet, sauté onion and garlic in butter until tender. Stir in tomatoes, seasonings, cauliflower and broccoli. Cook uncovered, until heated through, about 4 minutes, stirring occasionally. Remove from heat, set aside. In a large bowl, beat eggs and cream; stir in 1 cup of Swiss cheese, Parmesan cheese and the vegetable mixture. Transfer to a greased, shallow 2-quart baking dish. Sprinkle with remaining Swiss cheese. Bake uncovered for 25-30 minutes or until knife inserted in center comes out out clean. Let stand 10 minutes before serving. Reheats well. 12 servings

ELK RIVER CHICKEN MARINADE
(for grill)

- 1 cup vegetable oil
- 2 eggs
- 1 pint cider vinegar
- 1 tablespoon each salt and pepper
- 1 tablespoon poultry seasoning
- 1 teaspoon garlic salt
- 1 teaspoon dried oregano
- 1 teaspoon seasoning salt

Beat eggs with mixer. Add oil and beat until well blended. Add vinegar and seasonings and mix well. Marinate chicken for at least one hour—but longer is better. Use small chicken pieces such as legs and halved boneless breasts. Cook over low fire, brushing with sauce and turning often. Cook at least 45 minutes. Makes enough marinade for 15-25 small pieces of chicken.

FETTUCCINE
WITH SPINACH SAUCE

- 1 (16-ounce) package fettuccine
- 1 (10-ounce) package frozen, chopped spinach
- ¼ cup butter
- 1 cup Ricotta cheese
- ¼ cup grated Parmesan cheese
- ¼ cup whipping cream
- ½ teaspoon salt
- ⅛ teaspoon ground nutmeg

Cook fettuccine according to package directions; drain well. Rinse with warm water, and drain again; set aside. Cook spinach according to package directions; drain and set aside. Melt butter in a large skillet over medium heat. Add spinach, cheese, whipping cream, salt and nutmeg; stir well. Combine spinach mixture and warm fettuccine, tossing gently. 8-10 servings

FIESTA PORK BAKE

- 2 tablespoons butter, melted
- 6 rib pork chops
- salt and pepper to taste
- 1 package dry onion soup mix
- 1 large green pepper, chopped
- 1 cup uncooked regular rice
- ½ cup catsup
- 1 teaspoon Worcestershire sauce
- 2 cups boiling water
- 1 cup shredded cheddar cheese

Pre-heat oven to 350 degrees. Coat a shallow 2-quart casserole with melted butter. Sprinkle chops with salt and pepper and arrange in casserole; top with soup mix, green pepper and rice. Combine catsup with Worcestershire sauce; spread over rice. Pour in boiling water, cover and bake for 55-60 minutes or until done. An additional ½ cup water may be added if casserole becomes too dry. Remove from oven and top with cheese. Cover and allow to stand for 10 minutes. 6 serving

FISH BAKE

- 1 pound fresh fish (Cod, Halibut, Monk, Cat, Trout) filets
- 1 tablespoon flour per filet of fish
- 1 tablespoon cornmeal
- olive oil

Pre-heat oven to 400 degrees. Combine flour and cornmeal and dredge fish. Coat baking dish with olive oil (1 tablespoon per filet). Bake fish for 30 minutes or until golden brown.

Wash and pat dry potatoes (enough for 4 servings); cut into long quarters. Sprinkle generously with olive oil and bake until golden brown. Serve with salt and malt vinegar. 4 servings

GOAT CHEESE STUFFED CHICKEN BREASTS OVER ANGEL HAIR PASTA

- 3 ounces goat cheese, softened
- ½ cup chopped fresh basil
- ½ teaspoon pepper
- 4 skinless, boneless chicken breasts
- ½ teaspoon salt
- 8 large fresh basil leaves
- 8 ounces angel hair pasta, cooked
- Tomato-basil Sauce**

**Make tomato-basil sauce a day ahead, but stuff chicken on the day you serve it so basil leaves will stay fresh

Pre-heat oven to 350 degrees. Stir together first 3 ingredients. Place chicken breasts between two sheets of waxed paper and flatten to ¼-inch thickness with meat mallet. Sprinkle with salt; place 2 basil leaves and 2 tablespoons cheese mixture in center of each breast. Roll up, jellyroll fashion, starting with a short end, and secure with wooden picks. Place rolls, seam side down, in lightly greased 8-inch square pan. Bake for 30-35 minutes or until done; let stand for 10 minutes, and then cut into ½-inch slices. Toss pasta with half of tomato-basil sauce. Serve chicken over pasta, and top with remaining sauce. 4 servings

** Tomato-basil sauce

- 1 small onion
- 4 garlic cloves, chopped
- 2 tablespoons olive oil
- 1 cup dry red wine
- ½ teaspoon salt
- ¼ teaspoon pepper
- 2 (28-ounce) cans diced tomatoes
- ½ cup fresh basil leaves, shredded

In large saucepan sauté onion and garlic in hot oil until tender. Add dry red wine, salt and pepper and cook, stirring occasionally, 5 minutes. Add diced tomatoes, reduce heat, and simmer, stirring often for 30 minutes. Cool mixture slightly. Process half of tomato mixture in a blender or food processor until smooth; return to saucepan. Repeat procedure with remaining tomato mixture. Add to mixture in saucepan and cook over medium heat until sauce is thoroughly heated, stir in shredded basil. Makes 5 cups

GREEK PASTA SALAD WITH SHRIMP

- 1 pound spiral pasta, cooked as directed, rinsed in cold water and drained
- 1 pound cooked shrimp, halved lengthwise
- 8 to 10 ounces cherry tomatoes, halved
- 1 green pepper, diced
- ½ small red onion, diced
- 1 medium zucchini (or English cucumber) halved and sliced
- 1 (4-ounce) package Feta cheese with basil and sun-dried tomatoes
- 1 small can sliced black olives
- salt and pepper to taste

Mix all of the above and season to taste then add dressing, mix well, and chill until serving. 6-8 servings

Dressing:
- ¼ cup rice wine vinegar
- 2 tablespoons Dijon mustard
- 1 large clove of garlic, minced
- large pinch of salt
- black pepper to taste
- ⅔ cup extra-virgin olive oil

GREEN TOMATO PIE

- 6 cups sliced green tomatoes
- 1 cup sugar
- ¼ teaspoon salt
- 3 tablespoons flour
- ¼ teaspoon nutmeg
- ¼ teaspoon cinnamon
- ¼ teaspoon ground cloves
- grated rind & juice of 1 lemon
- 2 tablespoons butter
- Pastry for two-crust pie

Pre-heat oven to 450 degrees. Wash, but do not peel, tomatoes. Slice ⅛ inch thick. Cover with boiling water. Let stand 3 minutes. Drain. Combine sugar, salt, flour and spices. Fill pastry shell with layers of tomato, sprinkling each layer with sugar mixture. Cut second crust into strips and place in lattice pattern across top. Bake for 8-10 minutes. Reduce heat to 375 degree sand bake another 40 minutes. 4-6 servings

GRILLED SALMON STEAKS

- 4 fresh salmon steaks (about 1-inch thick)
- ½ cup lime juice
- 1 small onion, minced
- 2 to 3 green onions, minced
- ½ teaspoon each dry dill weed and grated lemon rind
- ¼ teaspoon freshly ground black pepper
- ¼ cup butter, melted

Lightly salt salmon. Mix next 5 ingredients to make marinade and place in a shallow dish. Marinate salmon steaks for 30 minutes. Drain and brush with butter. Take marinade and boil until volume is reduced by half. Place steaks in center of grill and cook 10 to 20 minutes until fish is tender and flakes with fork. Do not overcook. Turn salmon once and brush with the marinade halfway through cooking time. 4 servings

HAM AND TOMATO QUICHE

- 1 refrigerated piecrust prepared as directed using a 9-inch pie pan
- 1 cup diced cooked ham
- 1 medium tomato, thinly sliced
- 3 green onions, chopped
- 4 ounces shredded cheddar cheese
- 3 eggs
- ¾ cup milk
- 2 tablespoons flour
- ¼ cup Parmesan cheese

Preheat oven to 400 degrees. Layer ham, tomato, onion and cheddar cheese in prepared piecrust. In medium bowl, combine eggs, milk, flour and Parmesan cheese. Pour over layers in pan. Bake for 25-35 minutes or until golden brown and knife inserted in center comes out clean. If necessary, cover edge of crust with strips of foil after 15-20 minutes of baking to prevent excessive browning. Let stand 10 minutes before serving. 6 servings

HAM-CAULIFLOWER CASSEROLE

- 1 medium cauliflower cut into florets (about 3 cups)
- 4 tablespoons butter
- ⅓ cup all-purpose flour
- 1 cup milk
- 4 ounces (1 cup) shredded cheddar cheese
- ½ cup sour cream
- 2 cups cooked cubed ham
- 1 (3 or 4-ounce) can sliced mushrooms, drained
- 1 cup soft breadcrumbs
- 1 tablespoon cold butter

Pre-heat oven to 350 degrees. Cook cauliflower florets in boiling salted water for 10-12 minutes, or until tender. Drain and set aside. Melt 4 tablespoons butter in a medium saucepan over medium-high heat. Whisk in flour until smooth. Gradually add milk, whisking constantly, until mixture beings to thicken. Add cheese and sour cream, stirring until cheese melts. Do not boil. Stir in cauliflower, ham and mushrooms; pour into a 2-quart baking dish. Sprinkle breadcrumbs evenly over casserole. Cut 1 tablespoon butter into pieces and sprinkle evenly over breadcrumbs. Bake uncovered for about 45 minutes. 6 servings

HOPPING JOHN

- 1 pound package black-eyed peas
- 2 medium smoked ham hocks
- Seasonings: salt, bay leaf, cayenne pepper, garlic powder, Cajun spice
- 2 cups cooked white rice

Empty peas into a colander, rinse thoroughly in cold water and remove any defective peas. Place 2 hocks in a large pot and cover with about 3 inches of cold water. Cover the pot and place over a high flame. When water begins to boil add the peas and bay leaf. Lower flame. Season to taste with salt, cayenne pepper, garlic powder, Cajun spice. Replace lid. Stir periodically; add small amounts of water as needed. Cook until done (about an hour). Serve over cooked rice with chopped onion and hot sauce as condiments and corn bread. 8-10 servings

IMPOSSIBLE SEAFOOD PIE

- 6 ounces crabmeat, shrimp or tuna
- 1 cup shredded American cheese
- 3 ounces cream cheese, cut into about ¼-inch cubes
- ¼ cup thinly sliced green onions
- 2 cups milk
- 1 cup (Bisquick) baking mix
- 4 eggs
- ¾ teaspoon salt
- dash of nutmeg

Pre-heat oven to 400 degrees. Lightly grease a 10 x 1 ½-inch pie pan. Mix seafood with cheeses and onions and place in pie pan. Beat remaining ingredients until smooth. Pour into pie pan. Bake until knife inserted halfway between center and edge comes out clean, about 35-40 minutes. Let stand 5 minutes before serving. 6-8 servings

KIELBASA WITH KRAUT

- ½ cup chopped onion
- 2 slices of bacon, cut up
- 1 cup beer
- 1 cup water
- 2 tablespoons cornstarch
- 2 tablespoons brown mustard
- 2 tablespoons molasses
- ½ teaspoon allspice
- ¼ teaspoon pepper
- 1 large turnip, peeled and cut into 1-inch cubes
- 1 pound Kielbasa cut into 2 or 2 ½ inch pieces
- 1 or 2 medium tart apples cut in cubes or wedges
- 1 (14-ounce) can Bavarian sauerkraut (with caraway seeds), drained

In Dutch oven cook onion and bacon until tender, but not brown. Drain fat. Stir in beer. Mix water, cornstarch, mustard, molasses, allspice and pepper. Stir into bacon mixture and cook, stirring until thick and bubbly. Add turnip, cover and cook 15 minutes. Stir in Kielbasa, apples and sauerkraut. Cook, covered 15-20 minutes or until apples tender. 4 servings

LIGHT MACARONI AND CHEESE

- 1 ½ cups elbow macaroni
- 2 tablespoons vegetable oil
- ½ cup chopped green onion
- 1 garlic clove, minced
- 2 tablespoons all-purpose flour
- ¼ teaspoon dried basil
- ⅛ teaspoon black pepper
- 1 ¾ cups skim milk
- 4 ounces light Neufchatel cheese, softened, cubed
- 4 ounces sharp reduced-fat cheddar cheese, shredded
- 1 dash Tabasco sauce
- 1 tablespoon unseasoned dry bread crumbs

Pre-heat oven to 350 degrees. Oil 2-quart baking dish. Cook macaroni without salt until *al dente*, about 7 minutes. Drain well. Heat vegetable oil in large skillet on medium heat. Add onion and garlic and sauté until tender but not brown. Stir in flour, basil, pepper and Tabasco sauce. Blend well. Slowly blend in milk. Cook on medium heat, whisking constantly, until mixture thickens and bubbles. Add cheese. Stir until smooth. Add sauce to macaroni and mix well. Put into baking dish and sprinkle with breadcrumbs. Bake for approximately 25 minutes. 6 servings

LIVER AND ONIONS

- 1 pound beef liver, thinly sliced into serving pieces
- 3 tablespoons flour
- 4 medium yellow onions, thinly sliced
- ¼ cup water
- 2 tablespoons vegetable oil
- salt and pepper, to taste

Rinse liver and pat dry. Lightly coat in flour. In a large nonstick skillet cook onion in water, covered, over moderate heat for 3 minutes. Remove onion and reserve. Spray skillet with cooking spray and heat 1 tablespoon of oil over moderate heat. Add liver and cook for 2-3 minutes, until underside is brown. Turn liver, add remaining oil, cook for 2-3 minutes more. At last minute stir in onion and cook mixture, stirring, until heated through. Add salt and pepper to taste. 4 servings

MACARONI AND CHEESE

- 3 cups coarsely grated extra-sharp cheddar cheese (about 12 ounces)
- 1 ⅓ cups freshly grated Parmesan cheese (about 4 ounces)
- 7 tablespoons unsalted butter
- ¼ cup plus 2 tablespoons all-purpose flour
- 4 cups milk
- 1 ½ teaspoons dry mustard
- ⅛ teaspoon cayenne, or to taste
- salt and pepper to taste
- 1 pound elbow macaroni
- 1 cup fresh breadcrumbs

Pre-heat oven to 350 degrees and butter a 3 to 4-quart baking dish. In a heavy saucepan, melt 6 tablespoons butter over moderately low heat. Add flour and cook roux while whisking for 3 minutes. Add milk in a stream, whisking, and continue whisking until it comes to a boil. Add mustard, cayenne and salt and pepper to taste and simmer sauce, whisking occasionally, until thickened, about 2 minutes. Cook macaroni in a pot of salted boiling water until just al dente, about 7 minutes, and drain well. In a large bowl stir together macaroni, sauce, cheddar and 1 cup Parmesan and transfer to prepared dish. In a small bowl stir together breadcrumbs and remaining ⅓ cup Parmesan and sprinkle evenly over macaroni. Cut remaining 1 tablespoon butter into bits and scatter over the topping. Bake macaroni in middle of oven 25-30 minutes, or until golden and bubbling. 8 servings

MANICOTTI

- ½ pound ground beef
- 1 clove garlic, crushed
- 1 cup cottage cheese
- 4 ounces shredded Mozzarella cheese
- ½ teaspoon salt
- ½ cup mayonnaise
- 8 manicotti pasta cooked & drained
- 1 jar (16-ounces) marinara sauce
- ½ teaspoon dried oregano leaves
- Parmesan cheese

Pre-heat oven to 350 degrees. Brown beef and drain well. Mix next 4 ingredients in a bowl; stir in beef. Fill each manicotti with about ¼ cup cheese-meat mixture. Place in baking dish; cover with sauce. Sprinkle with oregano and Parmesan. Cover with foil. Bake for 15 minutes. Remove foil; bake 10 minutes longer. 4 servings

MARY ROSE'S TANDOORI CHICKEN

- 8 plumb chicken drumsticks, skin on

Marinade:
- 2 to 4 teaspoons Tandoori powder (Shan brand)*
- 4 tablespoons lemon juice
- 1 teaspoon salt

Pre-heat oven to 375 degrees. Make slits in chicken and coat both sides with marinade. Pour any remaining sauce over them, cover and refrigerate overnight. Spray foil lined pan with cooking spray and add chicken**. Dot with butter and bake for l hour.

*I purchase the powder in an Asian market and use only 2 teaspoons which is hot enough for me.

**May roll chicken in crushed cornflakes or breadcrumbs before baking (I don't). 4 servings

MEAT BALLS

- ½ pound ground round or chuck
- ¼ pound ground veal
- ¼ pound ground pork
- ¼ cup fresh breadcrumbs
- 3 tablespoons chopped fresh parsley
- 2 tablespoons grated Parmesan or Romano cheese
- 1 clove garlic, chopped fine
- salt, pepper to taste
- 2 tablespoons cooking oil
- ½ medium onion, chopped
- 1 pound fresh tomatoes, peeled, chopped, seeded (may use canned)
- ½ cup chicken stock

Combine meat, breadcrumbs, parsley, cheese, garlic and salt and pepper. Mix well and shape into small meatballs. In medium saucepan heat oil and sauté onion 3-4 minutes. Stir in tomatoes and cook a little longer (until tomatoes soft). Pour in broth and season lightly with salt and pepper. Add meatballs to pan, lower heat and cook 30-40 minutes, occasionally spooning sauce over meatballs. Serve over pasta. May be frozen, defrosted in refrigerator and warmed.

MONTE CRISTO

- 3 tablespoons Dijon mustard
- 6 tablespoons sour cream
- 12 slices good-quality white bread with fine texture
- 12 ounces thinly sliced Gruyere cheese
- 6 ounces thinly sliced Black Forest (or any good) ham
- 4 large eggs, beaten
- ½ cup butter

Mix mustard and sour cream and spread on bread. Cover half of slices with layers of cheese, ham and more cheese. Top with remaining bread, mustard sauce side down. Using hands, press sandwiches together firmly. Trim off crust and press down again. Dip both sides of sandwich in egg. In frying pan heat butter and cook sandwiches for 2-3 minutes per side, or until cheese is soft and sandwich is golden brown and crusty. 6 servings

MOUNTAINEER HASH

- 4 or 5 chopped ramps, stem and bulb
- 1 medium green pepper, chopped
- 3 tablespoons butter
- 1 pound ground beef
- 2 cups canned tomatoes
- 1 teaspoon chili powder
- ¼ teaspoon pepper
- 1 teaspoon salt
- 1 ½ cups uncooked rice

Pre-heat oven to 350 degrees. Sauté ramps and green pepper in butter until tender. Add ground beef and cook until all red is gone. Grease a baking dish and put ramps, green pepper and ground beef in casserole and add remaining ingredients, mixing well. Bake for 45 minutes. 4 servings

OLD FASHIONED MEAT LOAF

- 2 cups finely chopped onion
- 1 tablespoon minced garlic
- 1 celery rib, chopped fine
- 1 carrot, chopped fine
- ½ cup finely chopped scallions
- 2 tablespoons unsalted butter
- 2 teaspoons salt
- 1 ½ teaspoons pepper
- 2 teaspoons Worcestershire sauce
- ⅔ cup catsup
- 1 ½ pounds ground chuck
- ¼ pound ground pork
- 1 cup fresh breadcrumbs
- 2 large eggs, beaten lightly
- ⅓ cup dried parsley leaves

Preheat oven to 350 degrees. In large skillet cook onion, garlic, celery, carrot and scallion in butter over moderate heat, stirring about 5 minutes. Cook vegetables, covered, stirring occasionally until carrot is tender (about 5 minutes more). Stir in salt, pepper, Worcestershire sauce and ⅓ cup catsup and cook, stirring about 1 minute. In a large bowl combine vegetables, meats, breadcrumbs, eggs and parsley and mix well. In a shallow baking pan form mixture into a 10 x 5 oval loaf and spread remaining catsup over loaf. Bake meat loaf for about one hour or until done. 4-6 servings

ORANGE ROUGHY IN WINE

- ¼ cup white wine
- 4 Orange Roughy filets, about 6 ounces each
- 2 tablespoons olive oil
- 2 tablespoons fresh basil, chopped
- 1 teaspoon black pepper
- grated zest of 2 lemons

Preheat oven to 325 degrees. Pour wine into a baking dish large enough to hold all the filets in a single layer. Brush both sides of the filets with olive oil and lay in the baking dish. Combine basil, pepper and zest and sprinkle over filets. Bake 20-30 minutes, until fish flakes easily. 4 servings

OVEN BARBECUED SPARERIBS

- 3-4 pounds spareribs, cut into pieces
- 2 tablespoons butter
- 1 clove garlic, chopped
- 1 cup catsup
- 1 cup water
- 2 tablespoons lemon juice
- 1 tablespoon paprika
- 1 tablespoon Worcestershire sauce
- dash Tabasco sauce
- 2 onions, sliced
- 2 lemons, sliced

Preheat oven to 450 degrees. Place ribs in oven pan and roast until brown (about 30 minutes).

Drain fat from pan and set aside. Reduce oven temperature to 350 degrees.

Sauce:
Melt butter in saucepan, sauté garlic 1 minute, then add catsup, water, lemon juice, paprika, Worcestershire and Tabasco and blend well. Place onion and lemon slices over ribs and cover with sauce. Bake, basting occasionally, for 1½ hours. 4-6 servings

OVEN GARLIC CHICKEN

- 1 frying chicken cut into pieces
- ¾ cup all purpose flour
- 1 teaspoon salt
- 2 teaspoons garlic powder
- ¼ teaspoon pepper
- 1 tablespoon paprika
- 1 stick butter

Pre-heat oven to 400 degrees. Mix dry ingredients in heavy paper bag. Coat chicken evenly with seasoned flour. Melt butter in a 13 x 9 x 2-inch pan. Arrange chicken in single layer. Bake about 30 minutes. Baste chicken with butter from pan and bake another 15-20 minutes or until chicken is brown. 4-6 servings

PARMESAN HAM PASTA

- 1 (16-ounce) package bow-tie pasta
- 2 cups cubed fully cooked ham
- 1 (4-ounce) can mushroom stems and pieces or sliced, drained
- ½ cup butter
- ½ cup all-purpose flour
- ½ teaspoon salt
- 2 cups milk (not less than 2 percent milk)
- 1 (10-ounce) package frozen chopped spinach, partially thawed
- ½ cup shredded Parmesan cheese

Cook pasta according to package directions. Meanwhile, in a large skillet, sauté ham and mushrooms in butter. Stir in flour and salt until blended. Gradually add milk. Bring to a boil and cook, stirring constantly until thickened (about 2 minutes). Reduce heat. Stir in spinach and cheese. Cook and stir until cheese is melted. Drain pasta; stir in ham mixture. 6 servings

PASTA CASSEROLE

- 8 ounces penne, cooked al dente
- 6 ounces sliced ham, cut into ½-inch pieces
- 6 ounces sliced smoked turkey, cut into ¼-inch pieces
- 1 (10 ¾-ounce) can cheddar cheese soup
- ½ cup milk
- ¼ teaspoon pepper
- 8 tomato slices
- 8 slices of bacon, cooked
- ¼ cup shredded Parmesan cheese

Pre-heat oven to 350 degrees. Combine cooked penne and meats in a bowl. Combine soup, milk and pepper, and then stir into pasta mixture. Spoon into four lightly greased individual baking dishes; top with tomato slices. Bake for 15 minutes. Top with bacon and sprinkle with Parmesan cheese. Bake 5 minutes more or until cheese melts slightly. Serve immediately. 4 servings

PENNE AND SHRIMP
WITH YOGURT DILL DRESSING

- 16 ounces penne pasta
- 2 tablespoons butter
- 2 cloves garlic, minced
- 1 pound medium shrimp, shelled
- 1 cucumber, peeled, seeded and diced
- 3 tablespoons chopped fresh dill
- 3 or 4 scallions, chopped
- ¼ teaspoon paprika
- 1 ½ teaspoon salt
- ¼ teaspoon pepper
- 1 ½ cups plain yogurt
- ¼ cup mayonnaise

Cook pasta according to package directions. Rinse with cold water and drain thoroughly. In a medium frying pan, melt butter over moderate heat. Stir in the garlic, then the shrimp, ¼ teaspoon salt and the pepper. Cook, stirring until the shrimp are just done, about 4 minutes. Remove from the pan and set aside. In a large bowl combine the yogurt and remaining ingredients and 1 ¼ teaspoon salt. Toss pasta with yogurt sauce and shrimp/garlic mix. 6-8 servings

PENNE PASTA CASSEROLE

- 1 pound lean ground beef or ground turkey
- 1 large onion, chopped
- 1 (14.5 ounce) can diced tomatoes with basil, garlic and oregano
- 1 (6-ounce) can tomato paste
- 12 ounces (about 3 ½ cups) uncooked penne pasta prepared according to package directions
- 3 cups shredded Mozzarella cheese, divided
- ½ cup water

Pre-heat oven to 350 degrees. Cook ground beef/turkey with onion in a large skillet until done. Stir in diced tomatoes and tomato paste and ½ cup water. Season to taste; heat through. Coat a 9 x 13 x 2-inch baking dish with cooking spray. Combine cooked pasta with meat-tomato mixture, and 2 cups Mozzarella cheese. Place in baking dish and top evenly with remaining cheese. Bake uncovered for 20-25 minutes or until heated through and cheese is melted. 6-8 servings

PENNE WITH BROCCOLI

- ½ pound penne
- 1 (16-ounce) bag frozen broccoli cuts
- 1 pound jar of lite Alfredo sauce
- dried crushed red pepper flakes
- black pepper
- 4 tablespoons butter
- ¼ to ½ cup finely shredded Parmesan cheese (dairy packaged)
- 1 ½ to 2 cups cubed cooked ham or chicken (optional)

Cook penne according to package directions. While cooking, steam broccoli. Heat Alfredo sauce in a double boiler and add red pepper flakes and black pepper to taste. When pasta is done drain and mix with butter. Add Alfredo sauce, broccoli and Parmesan cheese and mix well. Add ham or chicken if desired. 4-6 servings

PENNE WITH MEATBALLS

- ½ pound penne
- 1 (14.5-ounce) can diced tomatoes with mild or hot chilies
- 1 (14.5-ounce) can diced tomatoes with green pepper and onion
- 12 frozen Italian meatballs, baked as directed and drained
- olive oil
- garlic powder
- butter
- Parmesan cheese

Cook penne as directed *al dente*. While pasta is cooking simmer canned tomatoes and garlic powder (to taste) until slightly thickened. Drain penne and toss lightly with butter and Parmesan. Add tomato sauce and meatballs, (cut into quarters) to pasta and mix well. Reheats well. 4 servings

ROAST PORK

- 4 pound pork loin roast
- salt and pepper to taste
- 1 teaspoon dried thyme
- 1 bay leaf, crumbled

Rub roast all over with the seasonings several hours ahead and refrigerate until ready to cook.

Pre-heat oven to 350 degrees. Place roast on a rack in an uncovered roasting pan and roast for about 2 ½ hours (about 40 minutes per pound). Baste frequently. 6 servings

PORK-POTATO KABOBS

- 2 pounds new potatoes
- ⅓ cup olive oil
- ¼ cup balsamic vinegar
- 6 garlic cloves, pressed
- 1 tablespoon dried rosemary, crushed
- 2 teaspoons each salt and pepper
- 2 (1-pound) pork tenderloins, cut into 2-inch pieces
- 2 red bell peppers, cut into 2-inch pieces

Cook new potatoes in boiling water; covered, for about 10 minutes or until tender. Drain, rinse with cold water and cut into fourths. Combine oil and next five ingredients in a shallow dish or large heavy-duty ziplock plastic bag. Reserve 3 tablespoons of marinade for vegetables. Add pork to original marinade, cover or seal, and chill for two hours, turning occasionally. Pour reserved marinade into a shallow dish or large zip-lock plastic bag; add potatoes and bell pepper. Cover or seal and chill two hours, turning occasionally. When ready to grill, remove pork and vegetables from marinades, discarding marinades. Thread pork and vegetables alternately onto skewers, leaving a ½-inch space between them. Grill, covered with grill lid, over medium-high heat of 350-400 degrees for 10-12 minutes turning occasionally, or until done. 6 servings

Grilling tip: Place food at least ¼ inch apart for even cooking. Also, sprinkling fresh or dried herbs on the coals just before grilling will add fragrance to the food and is a good way to use up "old" dried herbs.

POTATO HAM QUICHE

- 3 cups frozen shredded hash brown potatoes, thawed
- ¼ cup butter melted, divided
- ½ cup each shredded pepper-jack cheese and Swiss cheese
- 1 cup diced fully cooked ham
- 2 eggs
- ½ cup whipping cream
- ¼ teaspoon seasoned salt

Pre-heat oven to 425 degrees. Press hash browns between paper towel to remove excess moisture. Grease a 9-inch pie pan with 2 teaspoons melted butter. Press hash browns onto the bottom and up the sides of the pan. Drizzle with remaining melted butter. Bake uncovered at 425 degrees for 20-25 minutes or until edges are browned. Reduce oven to 350 degrees. Combine cheeses and ham; spoon onto crust. In a separate bowl, mix eggs, cream and seasoned salt until well-blended; pour over ham mixture. Bake at 350 degrees uncovered for 20-25 more minutes or until knife inserted near the center comes out clean. Let stand 10 minutes before slicing. 6 servings

RATATOUILLE PIE

- 1 cup chopped zucchini
- 1 cup chopped pared eggplant
- ½ cup chopped tomato
- ½ cup chopped green pepper
- ¼ cup chopped onion
- 1 medium clove garlic, crushed
- ¼ cup butter
- ¾ teaspoon salt
- ½ teaspoon dried basil
- ½ teaspoon dried thyme
- ⅛ teaspoon pepper
- 1 cup shredded Monterey Jack with jalapeno peppers
- 1 ¼ cup milk
- ¼ cup sour cream
- ¾ cup Bisquick
- 3 eggs

Pre-heat over to 400 degrees. Lightly grease a 10 x 1 ½-inch pie pan (or may use larger Pyrex dish and make thinner pie). Cook first 6 ingredients in butter, stirring occasionally, until vegetables are tender-crisp, about 10 minutes. Stir in seasonings and spread mixture in pie pan. Sprinkle with shredded cheese (may do up to this point and refrigerate, adding beaten ingredients just before baking). Beat remaining ingredients until smooth and pour over top of pie. Bake until knife inserted halfway between center and edge comes out clean (about 35 minutes). Reheats well. 4-6 servings

RED BEANS AND RICE

- 1 pound dried red beans
- 6 cups water
- 1 ½ pounds smoked sausage, sliced
- ½ pound thick cooked ham, cubed
- 1 large sweet onion, chopped
- 2 garlic cloves, pressed
- 2 tablespoons olive oil
- 1 bunch green onions, chopped
- 1 cup chopped fresh parsley
- 1 teaspoon salt
- 1 teaspoon pepper
- ½ teaspoon sugar
- ½ teaspoon dried oregano
- ½ teaspoon thyme
- ⅛ teaspoon ground red pepper (or more if desired)
- 1 tablespoon Worcestershire sauce
- ¼ teaspoon hot sauce (or to taste)
- hot cooked rice

Place beans in a large Dutch oven. Cover with 2 inches of water and soak overnight (or at least 8 hours). Drain. Bring beans, 6 cups water, sausage and ham to a boil in the Dutch oven. Cover, reduce heat, and simmer 3 hours. Sauté onion and garlic in hot oil in a large skillet until tender. Add to bean mixture. Stir in green onions and next 9 ingredients. Cover and chill overnight (or at least 8 hours). Bring bean mixture to a simmer; cover and cook, stirring often for 1 hour. Serve over hot rice. 8-10 servings

REUBEN CASSEROLE

- 2 cans (10 ¾-ounces each) cream of mushroom soup
- 1 ⅓ cups milk
- ½ cup chopped onion
- 1 tablespoon prepared mustard
- 2 cans (14 ½ to 16 ounces each) sauerkraut, rinsed and drained
- 1 (8-ounce) package medium-width noodles, uncooked
- 1 ½ pounds Polish sausage, cut into ½-inch pieces
- 2 cups shredded Swiss cheese
- ¾ cup whole wheat bread crumbs
- 2 tablespoons butter, melted

Preheat oven to 350 degrees. Combine soup, milk, onion and mustard in medium bowl; blend well. Spread sauerkraut in a greased 13 x 9-inch pan. Top with uncooked noodles. Spoon soup mixture evenly over this layer and top with sausage, then cheese. Combine crumbs and butter in small bowl and sprinkle over the top. Cover pan tightly with foil. Bake for 1 hour or until noodles are tender. 8-10 servings

RIGATONI WITH CHICKEN, BROCCOLI

- 2 tablespoons vegetable oil
- 1 pound boneless, skinless chicken breasts, cut into 1-inch cubes
- 2 cloves garlic, minced
- ⅛ teaspoon crushed red pepper
- 1 can (13.75 or 14.5-ounce) chicken broth
- 1 tablespoon corn starch
- ½ teaspoon salt
- ¼ teaspoon dried thyme
- 1 (10-ounces) package frozen chopped broccoli, thawed
- 16 ounces Rigatoni, cooked and drained

In a large skillet heat oil over medium heat. Add chicken, garlic and crushed red pepper and sauté 4 minutes or until chicken is lightly browned. In a small bowl stir broth, cornstarch, salt and thyme; add to skillet. Stir in broccoli. Bring to a boil over medium heat and boil 1 minute. Reduce heat to low; cook 4 minutes longer or until heated through. Toss with Rigatoni. 8 servings

RIGATONI WITH ZUCCHINI AND HAM

- 1 cup chicken broth
- 6 cups zucchini cut into ½-inch pieces
- 1 ½ tablespoons all- purpose flour
- 1 cup milk
- 1 pound cooked Rigatoni
- 5-8 ounces thick ham cut into cubes
- ½ cup plus teaspoons grated Parmesan cheese
- ¼ cup butter
- ½ teaspoon pepper
- salt
- dash of red pepper flakes

Bring chicken broth to a boil in a large skillet. Add zucchini and cook over medium heat 6-7 minutes, stirring often until crisp-tender. Whisk flour into milk and add to broth. Boil gently 1-2 minutes whisking constantly, until sauce slightly thickened. Pour sauce over pasta in pot. Add ham cubes, ½ cup Parmesan, butter, pepper, salt, and pepper flakes. Toss to mix and coat. Pour into serving bowls and sprinkle with remaining cheese. 6 servings

SALMON BURGERS

- 1 (14.75-ounce) can salmon
- 1 egg slightly beaten
- ½ cup chopped onions
- ½ cup finely chopped green pepper, fresh whole
- wheat (or white) breadcrumbs
- 1 tablespoon lemon juice
- 1 teaspoon grated lemon peel
- ½ teaspoon rosemary, crushed
- ⅛ teaspoon pepper

Drain salmon and flake. Combine all ingredients and mix well. Form into 4-5 patties. Pan fry in a small amount of vegetable oil until lightly brown on both sides. Serve on toasted hamburger buns with favorite condiments. 4-5 servings

SALMON LOAF

- 2 (6-ounce) cans boneless/skinless salmon
- 4 crushed saltine crackers
- 1 large shallot, chopped (or small onion)
- ¼ cup green pepper, chopped
- 1 egg
- pepper and celery salt to taste
- 1 tablespoon Worcestershire sauce
- 2 tablespoons catsup
- ¼ teaspoon hot pepper sauce
- dash dried celery flakes

Pre-heat oven to 350 degrees. Mix together first 4 ingredients. Beat egg with remaining ingredients except celery flakes. Mix all ingredients together and put in greased baking dish. Bake for about 30 minutes. 4-6 servings

SALMON QUICHE

Crust:
- 1 cup whole wheat flour
- ⅔ cup grated cheddar cheese
- ¼ cup chopped, toasted almonds
- pinch of salt
- ¼ teaspoon paprika
- 6 tablespoons salad oil

Pre-heat oven to 400 degrees. Combine dry ingredients, add oil, stir well and press into a 9-inch pie plate. Bake for 10 minutes and then cool.

Filling:
- 1 (6 ½-ounces) can salmon
- 3 eggs, beaten
- ½ cup sour cream
- ½ cup yogurt
- ¼ cup mayonnaise
- ½ cup grated cheddar cheese
- ¼ teaspoon chopped green onion
- ¼ teaspoon dill weed
- 3 drops hot pepper sauce (optional)

Pre-heat oven to 325 degrees. Drain and flake salmon, reserve the liquid. Blend eggs, sour cream, yogurt, mayonnaise and salmon liquid, then fold in salmon, cheese, onions, dill and hot pepper sauce. Spoon in shell and bake for about 40 minutes or until firm. 4-6 servings

SAUSAGE AND CABBAGE

- 1 (16-ounce) package Kielbasa sausage, cut into 1-inch pieces
- 1 medium onion, thinly sliced
- 1 green bell pepper, cut into strips
- 6 cups coarsely chopped cabbage
- 1 cup dry white wine or chicken broth
- ½ teaspoon caraway seeds
- ½ teaspoon salt
- ½ teaspoon pepper

Sauté sausage in a large skillet over medium heat until browned; drain on paper towels. Add onion and bell pepper to skillet, and sauté 2-3 minutes. Add cabbage, and cook, stirring often about 8 minutes. Add sausage, wine and remaining ingredients. Reduce heat to medium-low and cook 10 minutes or until cabbage is tender. 4 servings

SAUSAGE AND PEPPERS WITH CHEESE GRITS

- 1 (18 or 20 ounce) package sweet Italian sausage
- 3 bell peppers (red, yellow or green) seeded and cut into strips
- 1 large sweet onion, cut in half and thinly sliced
- 2 cloves garlic, minced
- 1-2 teaspoons Italian seasoning
- ½ teaspoon garlic powder
- 1 teaspoon salt
- ½ teaspoon pepper
- Parmesan cheese grits **
- extra Parmesan cheese, grated

Remove sausage casings and discard. Cook sausage and next 7 ingredients in a large skillet over medium-high heat, stirring until sausage crumbles and is no longer pink and vegetables are tender. Serve over grits and add extra Parmesan cheese, if desired.

** Parmesan cheese grits:
- 1 cup grits
- 4 cups water
- ¾ teaspoon salt
- 1 tablespoon butter
- 5 ounces of shredded Parmesan cheese

Cook grits according to package directions, using 4 cups water. Stir in salt, butter and Parmesan cheese. 4 servings

SAVORY STUFFED CABBAGE

- 8 large cabbage leaves
- 1 (10 ¾-ounce) can tomato soup
- 1 pound ground chuck
- 1 cup cooked rice
- ¼ cup chopped onion
- 1 egg, slightly beaten
- 1 teaspoon salt
- ¼ teaspoon pepper

Cook rice and reserve. Cook cabbage in salted water a few minutes to soften. Remove 8 large leaves. Drain. Mix 2 tablespoons soup with rest of ingredients and divide mixture between cabbage leaves. Fold up sides, roll up and secure with toothpicks. Place cabbage rolls, seam side down in a large skillet and cover with remaining soup. Cover; simmer 40 minutes stirring now and then and spooning sauce over rolls. 4 servings

SCALLOPS CREOLE

- 1 pound fresh bay scallops
- 2 cans (14 ½-ounces each) canned tomatoes
- 1 medium onion, chopped
- 1 (4-ounce) can mushrooms
- chili powder, minced garlic cloves, dried thyme, dried basil,
- salt and pepper to taste

Mix all ingredients except scallops and rice and simmer about 15 minutes. Then add 1 pound fresh bay scallops. Cook until done (about 30 minutes) or until sauce thickens. Serve over rice. 4 servings

SCALLOPS WITH
ANGEL HAIR PASTA

- ½ cup hot water
- ¼ cup chopped dried tomatoes
- 1 small onion, chopped
- 2 cloves garlic, minced
- 2 tablespoons olive oil
- 1 small green bell pepper, chopped
- 1 medium red bell pepper, chopped
- 1 pound bay scallops, drained
- 1 cup half-and-half
- ¼ teaspoon salt
- ¼ teaspoon dried red pepper flakes (optional)
- 8 ounces angel hair pasta, cooked
- ½ cup grated Parmesan cheese

Pour ½ cup hot water over tomatoes. Let stand 10 minutes or until softened. Drain and set aside. Sauté onion and garlic in hot oil in a large skillet over medium heat until tender. Add tomatoes and bell peppers and sauté 3-4 minutes or until tender. Reduce heat to low; stir in scallops, half-and-half, salt, and if desired, dried red pepper flakes. Cook, stirring often, 2-3 minutes or until scallops are opaque. Toss together pasta and scallop mixture. Sprinkle with Parmesan. 4 servings

SEAFOOD LASAGNE ROLLUPS

- 6 lasagne noodles
- 1 (16-ounce) jar Italian style tomato sauce (marinara)

Filling:
- 1 package imitation crabmeat
- 1 cup low fat cottage cheese, drained
- ¼ cup grated Parmesan cheese
- 1 egg
- 1 tablespoon dried parsley flakes
- ¼ teaspoon onion powder

Pre-heat oven to 375 degrees. Cook noodles as directed on package. Rinse in cold water and drain well. Combine filling ingredients with fork. Spread ⅓ cup filling on each noodle Roll tightly; place seam side down in a 9-inch baking dish. Pour sauce over rollups. Bake covered for 30 minutes. Garnish with grated cheese. 6 servings

SHELLS WITH GREENS

- 8 ounces of shell pasta, cooked
- 5 slices bacon
- 2 cloves of garlic, minced
- 1 medium onion, chopped
- 1 tablespoon Dijon mustard
- 1 (10-ounce) package frozen / chopped collard greens, thawed & drained
- 1 (14 ½-ounce) can diced tomatoes (I use the one with Italian seasonings)
- ¼ teaspoon pepper
- shredded (or canned) Parmesan cheese

Cook bacon in a large skillet until crisp; remove bacon, reserving 1 tablespoon of drippings in the skillet. Crumble bacon and set aside. Sauté garlic and onion in drippings until tender. Add mustard, collard greens and tomatoes. Reduce heat to medium and cook about 10 minutes. Add pepper to tomato mixture and toss mixture with pasta to coat. Top with crumbled bacon and Parmesan cheese. 4 serving

SHRIMP AND ARTICHOKE QUICHE

- ¾ pound frozen cooked shrimp, thawed and coarsely chopped (about 1 ½ cups)
- 3 green onions, sliced
- 4 ounces shredded Swiss cheese
- 4 ounces shredded Parmesan cheese
- 1 cup baking mix
- 2 large eggs
- 1 cup milk
- 1 ½ teaspoons Cajun seasoning
- 1 (14-ounce) can small artichoke hearts, drained and cut in half lengthwise

Pre-heat oven to 400 degrees. Sprinkle shrimp and green onions in a lightly greased 9-inch pie pan. Combine Swiss and Parmesan cheese; sprinkle half of cheese mixture evenly over shrimp mixture. Whisk together baking mix and next 3 ingredients until blended. Pour evenly over cheeses in pie pan; top with artichoke heart halves, cut sides down, and remaining cheese mixture. Bake for 30-35 minutes or until knife inserted in center comes out clean. Let stand 10 minutes before serving. 6-8 servings

SHRIMP AND LINGUINE

- 1 pound medium shrimp
- 5 green onions, sliced
- 3 cloves garlic, minced
- 2 tablespoons olive oil
- 1 (12-ounce) jar marinated artichoke hearts, un-drained
- 6 plum tomatoes, chopped
- 1 cup sliced fresh mushrooms
- ¼ cup dry white wine
- 2 teaspoons dried Italian seasoning
- ¼ teaspoon rosemary, crushed
- ¼ teaspoon each salt, pepper
- cooked linguine
- Parmesan cheese

If using fresh shrimp, peel and de-vein. Sauté green onions and garlic in olive oil in a large skillet until tender. Stir in artichoke hearts and next seven ingredients. Bring to a boil; reduce heat and simmer five minutes. Add shrimp. If using fresh, cook, stirring occasionally, about three minutes or until shrimp turn pink. Serve over pasta and sprinkle with grated Parmesan. 4 servings

SHRIMP AND RICE CASSEROLE

- 1 pound cooked, peeled, de-veined shrimp
- 2 cups whole tomatoes, chopped
- 3 cups cooked rice
- 1 green pepper, cut into 1-inch strips
- 2 teaspoon salt
- ¼ teaspoon garlic powder

Pre-heat oven to 350 degrees. Combine all ingredients, mixing well. Spoon mixture into a greased 1 ¾ quart casserole. Bake for 35 minutes. 4 servings

SHRIMP WITH ROASTED RED PEPPER SAUCE

- 7 ounces of spaghetti
- 12 ounces of jarred roasted red peppers, drained
- 8 ounces of low fat cream cheese, softened
- ½ cup low sodium, fat-free chicken stock
- 3 garlic cloves, chopped
- ½ teaspoon ground red pepper
- 2 pounds cooked, peeled and de-veined large shrimp
- ¼ cup chopped fresh basil

Prepare spaghetti according to package directions but omitting salt and oil. Keep warm. Process red peppers and next 4 ingredients in a blender or food processor until smooth. Pour mixture into a large skillet and cook over medium heat about 5 minutes, stirring often, until heated thoroughly. Add shrimp, and cook, stirring occasionally 2-3 minutes or until heated. Pour over hot cooked pasta and sprinkle with fresh basil. 6 servings

SICILIAN SUPPER

- 1 pound ground chuck
- ½ cup chopped onion
- 1 (6-ounce) can tomato paste
- ¾ cup water
- 1 teaspoon salt
- ¼ teaspoon garlic powder
- 1 (8-ounce) package cream cheese
- ¾ cup milk
- ⅓ cup grated Parmesan cheese
- ¼ teaspoon salt
- 2 cups wide noodles, cooked and drained
- ½ cup chopped green pepper
- 1 tablespoon butter

Pre-heat oven to 350 degrees. Brown meat and drain. Add onion and cook until tender. Stir in tomato paste, water, salt and garlic powder. Simmer 5 minutes. In separate large skillet sauté green pepper in butter. Add cream cheese, milk and stir until cream cheese melts. Stir in Parmesan cheese, salt and noodles. In a 10 x 6-inch baking dish arrange alternate layers of meat mixture and noodles. Bake for 20 minutes (or until thoroughly heated). 6-8 servings

SLOW COOKER BEEF BARBECUE

- 2 or 2 ½ pound boneless chuck roast, trimmed
- 2 medium onions, chopped
- ¾ cup cola carbonated beverage
- ¼ cup Worcestershire sauce
- 1 tablespoon apple cider vinegar
- 2 cloves garlic, minced
- 1 teaspoon beef bouillon granules
- ½ teaspoon each dry mustard, chili powder
- ¼ teaspoon ground red pepper
- ½ cup catsup
- 2 teaspoons butter
- 6 hamburger buns

Combine roast and chopped onion in a 4-quart slow cooker. Combine cola and next 7 ingredients; reserve ½ cup in refrigerator. Pour remaining mixture over roast and onion in slow cooker. Cook, covered on high 6 hours or until roast in very tender; drain and shred roast.

Keep warm. Combine reserved ½ cup cola mixture, catsup and butter in a small saucepan; cook mixture over medium heat, stirring constantly, until thoroughly heated. Pour over shredded roast, stirring until mixed. Spoon onto buns and serve. 6 servings

SNAPPY CHICKEN AND NOODLES

- 1 (8-ounce) package wide egg noodles
- 1 teaspoon dried thyme leaves, crumbled
- 16 ounces fresh mushrooms, sliced
- 2 teaspoons (jarred) minced garlic
- 1 (10 ¾-ounce) can cream of mushroom soup
- ⅓ cup dry white wine (if not using, increase milk to 1 ⅓ cups)
- 1 rotisserie chicken, cut into serving pieces
- 2 tablespoons chopped fresh Italian parsley
- ½ teaspoon salt
- ¼ teaspoon pepper
- 3 tablespoons butter
- 1 large onion, chopped
- 1 cup milk
- 1 teaspoon paprika

Prepare noodles according to package directions. Keep warm. Meantime, stir together paprika, dried thyme, salt and pepper in a small bowl. Melt butter in a large skillet over medium heat; add onion and mushrooms, and sauté 8-10 minutes or until onion tender. Stir in garlic and paprika mixture; sauté 2 minutes. Add soup, milk, wine, and bring to a boil, stirring frequently. Add chicken pieces; spoon sauce over top of chicken. Reduce heat to low and cook, covered, 10-15 minutes or until chicken thoroughly heated. Stir in 1 tablespoon parsley. Serve over hot noodles. Sprinkle dish with remaining parsley. 4 servings

SOUR CREAM CHICKEN

- 1 chicken, cut into pieces
- ½ pint sour cream
- 2 tablespoons lemon juice
- 2 teaspoons Worcestershire sauce
- 1 package Pepperidge Farm herb stuffing mix rolled into fine crumbs
- 1 teaspoon celery salt
- 1 teaspoon paprika
- ½ teaspoon garlic salt
- ½ stick melted butter
- salt and pepper to taste

Pre-heat oven to 350 degrees. Mix sour cream and rest of ingredients (except stuffing mix). Coat pieces of chicken in mixture and then roll in stuffing crumbs. Arrange in shallow baking dish and brush with melted butter. Bake uncovered about 1 hour or until chicken tender and brown. 6-8 servings

SPAGHETTI CASSEROLE

- 8 ounces spaghetti
- 2 cups shredded Mozzarella cheese
- 12 ounces marinara sauce
- 1 pound ground beef
- 8 ounces sour cream
- 8 ounces pepperoni, chopped
- 6 green onions, chopped

Pre-heat oven to 400 degrees. Brown ground beef and 3 chopped onions. Drain fat. Stir in marinara sauce. Simmer 20 minutes. Prepare spaghetti according to package directions, drain. Put spaghetti in bottom of lightly creased casserole. Cover spaghetti with sour cream. Sprinkle remaining green onions over sour cream. Put marinara sauce over top of dish and sprinkle with chopped pepperoni. Bake for 20 minutes. Sprinkle cheese over the top and bake for an additional 10 minutes. 6-8 servings

SPAGHETTI WITH GRILLED VEGGIES

- 2 yellow squash
- 2 zucchini
- 1 small eggplant
- 1 purple onion
- 1 red bell pepper
- ⅓ cup butter, melted
- 2 - 3 teaspoons dried Italian seasonings
- 8 ounces uncooked spaghetti
- ¼ cup fresh grated Parmesan
- ½ teaspoons pepper
- 2 teaspoon chicken bouillon granules
- 2 quarts water

Cut squash, zucchini and eggplant into chunks; cut onion and bell pepper into fourths. Toss vegetables with butter and sprinkle with Italian seasoning and pepper. Grill vegetables, covered with grill lid, over high heat (400-500 degrees) for 20-30 minutes or until tender, turning occasionally. Remove from grill; keep warm. Bring 2 quarts of water to a boil and stir in chicken bouillon granules. Add spaghetti and cook until *al dente* (about 7 minutes). Drain. Top with the warm grilled vegetables and sprinkle with fresh grated Parmesan. 4 servings

SPAGHETTI WITH RAMP SAUCE

- ½ cup trimmed and minced ramps
- ½ teaspoon red pepper flakes
- ½ cup olive oil
- ½ pound spaghetti, cooked in boiling salted water until it is *al dente*

In a heavy skillet cook the ramps with the red pepper flakes in the oil over moderately low heat, stirring until they are softened and then increase heat to moderate and stir until ramps are golden. Add the spaghetti and salt and pepper to taste, toss the mixture until the spaghetti is coated with the sauce and transfer it to a serving bowl. 4 servings

SPANISH BEANS

- 1 pound of hot sausage
- 3 cans (14-ounces) lima beans, drained
- 1 can (14 ½-ounce) stewed tomatoes
- 1 cup chopped onion
- ½ cup chopped green pepper
- ½ cup chopped celery
- 2 tablespoons brown sugar
- 1 tablespoon chili powder

Pre-heat oven to 400 degrees. Fry sausage and pour off all but 3 tablespoons grease. Sauté onion, green pepper and celery in fat until tender. Break up tomatoes and combine with other ingredients and seasonings. Bake in covered casserole for 30 minutes. 6-8 servings

SPINACH CASSEROLE

- 2 pounds ground round beef
- ¼ pound fresh mushroom (about 5-6) thinly sliced
- 2 cloves garlic, minced
- 1 teaspoon dried oregano
- 2 (10-ounce) packages frozen chopped spinach (thawed in package)
- 1 (10 ¾-ounce) can cream of celery soup
- 1 (16-ounce) container of sour cream, at room temperature
- 1 teaspoon salt, ½ teaspoon pepper
- ½ cup coarsely shredded Mozzarella cheese (8-ounce package)
- Cooked noodles (optional)

Pre-heat oven to 350 degrees. Brown beef in large skillet and drain most of fat. Add mushrooms, garlic and oregano and sauté until mushrooms lightly browned. Add thawed spinach and heat until juices cooked away (about 10 minutes). Stir in soup, sour cream, salt and pepper. Lightly butter a 3-quart casserole and cover bottom with noodles (if using), spoon in spinach mixture and cover top with shredded cheese. Bake uncovered for 30 minutes or until bubbly. 6 servings

SPINACH LASAGNE

- 1 pound lean ground beef
- 1 large onion, minced
- ½ pound fresh mushrooms, sliced
- 1 teaspoon oregano
- ½ teaspoon basil leaves
- 1 ½ teaspoons salt, divided
- ¼ teaspoon pepper
- 1 (12-ounce) can cocktail vegetable juice
- 1 cup milk
- ½ cup all-purpose flour
- 1 cup cottage cheese
- 2 eggs
- 2 (10-ounce) packages frozen chopped spinach, thawed
- 1 (8-ounce) package lasagne noodles
- 1 (8-ounce) package Mozzarella cheese, thinly sliced
- 2 tablespoons grated Parmesan cheese
- fresh chopped Italian parsley

Pre-heat oven to 375 degrees. Cook ground beef until brown, stirring to crumble meat. Add onion, mushrooms, oregano, basil, 1 teaspoon salt, and pepper; cook until vegetables are tender. Stir in vegetable juice. Combine milk and flour; mix well, and stir into skillet mixture. Cook, stirring constantly, until thick and bubbly. Combine cottage cheese and 1 egg; mix well, and set aside. Drain spinach well. Combine spinach, 1 egg, and remaining ½ teaspoon salt; mix well, add cottage cheese mixture, half of cheese slices, and half of meat mixture. Spread evenly in a greased 13 x 9 x 2-baking dish. Layer half of noodles, half spinach; repeat layers. Sprinkle with Parmesan cheese; bake for 30 minutes. Sprinkle lightly with parsley. 6-8 servings

SPINACH NOODLE CASSEROLE

- 2 (10-ounce) packages frozen chopped spinach
- 2 cups uncooked medium egg noodles
- ¼ cup butter
- ¼ cup all purpose flour
- 2 cups milk
- ½ teaspoon salt
- ¼ teaspoon pepper
- 2 cups shredded cheddar or Colby cheese
- ¼ cup grated Parmesan cheese

Pre-heat oven to 350 degrees. Cook spinach according to package directions; drain well, and set aside. Cook noodles according to package directions; drain and set aside. Melt butter in a heavy saucepan over low heat; add flour, stirring until smooth. Cook 1 minute, stirring constantly. Gradually add milk, cook over medium heat, stirring constantly, until thickened and bubbly. Stir in salt and pepper. Stir ½ cup white sauce into spinach; spoon spinach mixture into a greased 9-inch square baking dish. Sprinkle with cheddar/Colby cheese. Combine noodles and ½ cup white sauce; spoon over cheese. Spoon remaining white sauce over noodles; sprinkle with Parmesan cheese. Bake uncovered for 30 minutes or until bubbly. 6 servings

SPINACH QUICHE

- 1 frozen piecrust baked as directed on package
- 4 eggs
- ¾ cup half-and-half
- salt and pepper to taste
- 2 tablespoons fresh parsley, minced (or dried if must)
- 2 tablespoons lemon juice
- 1 (10-ounce) box frozen spinach defrosted and all liquid squeezed out
- 4-6 ounces Feta cheese, crumbled
- grated Romano or Parmesan

Pre-heat oven to 375 degrees. Cook spinach according to package directions; drain well, and set aside. Mix eggs, half-an-half, seasonings, parsley and lemon juice until well blended. Stir in spinach and place all ingredients in baked piecrust.Sprinkle with Romano and bake about 30-40 minutes at 375 degrees. 4 servings

SPINACH STUFFED SHELLS

- 24 jumbo macaroni shells
- 1 (32-ounce) jar spaghetti sauce with mushrooms
- 1 (10-ounce) package frozen chopped spinach, thawed and drained
- 2 cups Ricotta cheese
- 2 cups (8-ounces) shredded Mozzarella cheese
- 1 small onion, diced
- ½ cup grated Parmesan cheese
- 2 tablespoons chopped fresh parsley
- 1 teaspoon dried oregano
- dash hot sauce
- dash ground nutmeg
- ¼ cup grated Parmesan cheese

Pre-heat oven to 350 degrees. Cook macaroni shells according to package directions; drain and set aside. Spoon 1 cup spaghetti sauce into a lightly greased 13 x 9 x 2-inch baking dish. Combine next 9 ingredients; mix well. Stuff each shell with 1 ½ tablespoons spinach mixture and arrange in baking dish. Spoon remaining spaghetti sauce over shells, sprinkle with Parmesan. Cover and bake for 30-40 minutes. 6-8 servings

STEAK KEBABS

- 2 tablespoons soy sauce (reduced sodium)
- 2 tablespoons honey
- 1 tablespoon grated fresh ginger or 1 teaspoon ground ginger
- 1 clove garlic, crushed
- 1 teaspoon grated lemon peel
- ¼ teaspoon crushed red pepper flakes
- 12 ounces boneless sirloin steak, trimmed and cut into 1-inch cubes
- 8 cherry tomatoes
- 4 large mushrooms, cut in half
- 1 green pepper, cored, seeded and cut into 8 squares

In a shallow glass dish combine first 6 ingredients and mix well. Add beef, stir to coat. Cover with plastic wrap and refrigerate for 1-2 hours, stirring occasionally. Preheat broiler. Remove beef from marinade. Discard marinade. Using 4 (10-inch) metal skewers, alternately thread beef, tomatoes, mushrooms and pepper.** Place on broiler pan. Broil 2 inches from heat, turning 2-3 times until meat is medium rare and vegetables are lightly brown (about 10 minutes).

**May be prepared and assembled up to 1 day in advance. Cover with plastic wrap and refrigerate until ready to cook. And of course, may do on your grill. 4 servings

STIR FRY BEEF AND VEGETABLES

- 3 tablespoon corn oil
- 2 cups broccoli florets
- 2 cups cauliflower florets
- 1 sweet red pepper, cut into 1-inch squares
- 1 pound tender beef steak, cut into thin strips
- 1 cup stir fry sauce mix

In wok or large skillet heat 2 tablespoons corn oil over medium high heat. Add broccoli, cauliflower and stir-fry 3 minutes. Add red pepper and stir-fry 1 minute. Remove vegetables from pan and add 1 tablespoon corn oil and the beefsteak. Stir-fry 3 minutes or until beef is brown. Return vegetables to pan and stir in 1 cup stir-fry sauce. Stirring constantly, bring to a boil over medium heat for 1 minute. 4 servings

Serve over rice.

STIR FRY CHICKEN AND VEGETABLES

- 2 tablespoons corn oil
- 1 ½ cups sliced carrots
- 2 green peppers, cut into ½-inch squares
- 2 onions, cut into ½-inch squares
- 1 tablespoon corn oil
- 1 pound boneless, skinless chicken breasts, cut into thin strips
- 1 cup stir fry sauce mix

In wok or large skillet heat 2 tablespoons of corn oil over medium-high heat. Add the carrots, peppers and onions and stir-fry 3 minutes. Remove from pan and add 1 tablespoon corn oil and chicken strips; stir-fry 2 minutes or until chicken turns white. Return vegetables to pan and stir in 1 cup stir fry sauce. Mix, stirring constantly, bring to boil over medium heat and boil 1 minute. Serve over rice. 4 servings

STIR FRIED SHRIMP AND SNOW PEAS

- 2 tablespoons corn oil
- 8 ounces sliced mushrooms
- 4 ounces trimmed snow peas
- 1 cup mung bean sprouts
- ½ cup green onions, sliced
- 1 tablespoon corn oil
- 1 pound shrimp, shelled and de-veined
- 1 cup stir-fry sauce mix

In wok or large skillet heat 2 tablespoons corn oil over medium high heat. Add the mushrooms, snow peas, bean sprouts and green onions and stir-fry 2 minutes. Remove vegetables from pan and add 1 tablespoon corn oil and stir fry shrimp 2 minutes or until shrimp turns pink. Return vegetables to the pan and stir in 1 cup stir-fry sauce mix. Stirring constantly, bring to boil over medium heat and boil 1 minute. Serve over rice. 4 servings

STUFFED ZUCCHINI SHELLS

- 3 medium zucchini
- 1 clove garlic, minced
- 2 tablespoons onion, chopped
- ½ cup fresh tomato, chopped
- ½ cup rice, cooked
- ¼ teaspoon oregano leaves
- ¼ teaspoon pepper

Preheat oven to 350 degrees. Wash zucchini and trim ends. Cut in half, lengthwise, and parboil in a small amount of boiling water for 5 minutes. Remove from water. Scrape out pulp and cube. Set aside zucchini shells. Spray a non-stick skillet with cooking spray. Add garlic and onion and cook until tender. Mix in tomato, rice, cubed zucchini, oregano and pepper. Stuff zucchini shells with mixture. Place stuffed shells on a baking sheet and bake for 30 minutes. 6 servings

SWEET AND SOUR MEATBALLS

- 1 pound ground lean beef
- 1 egg
- 1 tablespoon cornstarch

- ¼ cup (or more) chopped onions
- salt and pepper to taste

Sauce:
- 1 tablespoon vegetable oil
- 1 cup pineapple juice
- 3 tablespoons cornstarch
- 1 teaspoon soy sauce
- 3 teaspoon white vinegar

- 6 teaspoons water
- ½ cup sugar
- 1 large can pineapple chunks
- 2 large green peppers cut into lengthwise strips

Mix meatball ingredients and form into 1 or 1 ½ inch balls. Brown in small amount of oil until done, drain on paper towels. In another pan mix oil and pineapple juice. Bring to a boil. Mix cornstarch, Soy sauce, vinegar, water and sugar and add to pineapple juice, cooking and stirring until thickened. Add meatballs, pineapple chunks, green pepper strips to sauce and mix to coat all pieces with sauce. Heat and serve over cooked rice. 6-8 servings

SWEET AND SOUR PORK

- 1 (20-ounce) can pineapple chunks
- 2 tablespoons cornstarch
- ¼ cup soy sauce
- 1 tablespoon honey
- ½ teaspoon instant chicken bouillon granules
- 1 garlic clove, minced

- ⅛ teaspoon pepper
- 2 tablespoons vegetable oil
- ¾ pound pork tenderloin, cut into bite-size pieces
- 1 medium green pepper, thinly sliced
- hot cooked rice

Drain pineapple, reserving the juice; set pineapple aside. Add enough water to juice to equal ¾ cup. Add cornstarch, soy sauce, honey, bouillon, garlic and pepper; set aside. Heat oil in a large skillet (or wok) and cook and stir pork and green pepper for 6-8 minutes or until pork is no longer pink and green pepper is crisp-tender. Stir pineapple juice mixture into skillet with pineapple. Cook until sauce thickened and bubbly. Serve mixture over hot cooked rice. 4 servings

SWEET AND SOUR SKILLET PORK

- 1 pound boneless pork, cut into ¾-inch cubes
- 1 tablespoon vegetable oil
- 1 (20-ounce) can pineapple chunks
- ¼ cup vinegar
- 1 ½ teaspoon salt
- ½ teaspoon garlic salt
- 2 tablespoons sugar
- 1 cup regular uncooked rice
- l medium green pepper, halved, seeded and cut into small squares
- 1 medium tomato, cored and cut into thin wedges

Brown pork in oil in a 10-inch skillet and drain off fat. Drain juice from pineapple into a 4-cup glass measure; add water to make 2 ½ cups liquid. Add to skillet with vinegar, salt, garlic salt and sugar; bring to boil. Lower heat; cover; simmer 20 minutes. Stir in rice, recover and cook about 25 minutes or until liquid absorbed and pork tender. Add pineapple, green pepper and tomato wedges; heat thoroughly. 4 servings

SWEET VIDALIA ONION QUICHE

- 1 package refrigerated piecrust
- 2 large Vidalia onions, thinly sliced
- ¼ cup butter, melted
- 1 tablespoon molasses
- ⅓ cup half-and-half
- 2 large eggs
- ½ teaspoon salt
- pinch of white pepper
- ½ cup shredded Gruyere cheese (or aged Swiss, but it's not quite as sharp)

Pre-heat oven to 375 degrees. Unfold piecrust and place in fluted quiche pan or large pie pan. Bake according to package instructions and cool on wire rack. Toss onions with butter and molasses in a large shallow pan. Bake for 30 minutes, stirring every 10 minutes, until caramelized. Spoon onion mixture into piecrust. Whisk together half-and-half, eggs, salt and white pepper; pour over onion mixture. Place quiche on baking sheet and sprinkle with cheese. Bake for 20-25 minutes until onion quiche is golden. 4 servings

SWISS CHICKEN CUTLETS

- 2 thin slices of Swiss cheese (may use reduced fat)
- 4 chicken cutlets (about 4 ounces each)
- ¼-inch thick or may use boneless chicken breasts that have been pounded between sheets of wax paper to ¼-inch thickness
- 2 tablespoons all-purpose flour
- ½ teaspoon black pepper
- 1 tablespoon butter
- ½ cup chicken broth
- ¼ cup dry white wine or chicken broth
- ¼ teaspoon dried oregano
- chopped fresh parsley for garnish

Cut each cheese slice in half; place 1 half on top of each cutlet. Start with a short end and tightly roll up cutlets, jellyroll style. Tie securely with string. On waxed paper, combine flour and pepper. Mix well. Add cutlets; toss gently to coat. In a large non-stick skillet melt butter over medium heat. Add cutlets, cook, turning frequently, until golden, about 3 minutes. Add broth, wine and dried oregano to skillet. Increase heat; bring to a boil. Reduce heat to medium low; simmer until chicken is cooked through and sauce is slightly thickened, about 10-12 minutes. Place on a serving plate, remove string. Garnish with parsley. 4 servings

TACO SALAD PIE

- 1 packaged refrigerator piecrust
- 1 pound lean ground beef
- 1 (15-ounce) can spicy chili beans, un-drained
- ½ cup salsa (mild or hot to taste)
- 1 ½ cups shredded cheddar cheese
- 1 cup chopped lettuce
- ½ cup chopped tomato
- 1 green onion, diced
- ½ cup sour cream
- ¼ cup sliced ripe olives (optional)

Preheat oven to 450 degrees. Unfold piecrust and place in 9-inch pie pan. Prick bottom and sides with fork. Fork flute edge. Cut 13 (2-inch) triangle pieces from remaining crust, place around crust edge. Bake for 9-11 minutes or until light golden brown. Cool.

In a large skillet, brown ground beef and drain. Add chili beans, salsa and 1 cup cheese, mix well. Cook over low heat for 2-3 minutes or until beans are heated and cheese melted. Spoon into pie shell. Top with lettuce, remaining ½ cup cheese, tomato, onion, sour cream and olives. Serve immediately. 8 servings

THREE BEAN HOT DISH

- 1 ½ pounds ground chuck
- ½ cup chopped bacon
- ½ cup chopped onion
- 1 cup brown sugar
- 1 cup catsup
- 1 teaspoon prepared mustard
- 1 (15-ounce) can butter beans, drained
- 1 (15-ounce) can lima beans, drained
- 1 (15-ounce) can kidney beans, drained

Pre-heat oven to 350 degrees. Cook chopped bacon until crispy. Add ground chuck and onion and cook until beef brown and onion golden. Drain off excess grease. Mix brown sugar, catsup and mustard in large bowl and add meat mixture and the 3 cans of beans, stirring well. Place in casserole and bake, covered, for one hour. 8-10 servings

THREE CHEESE FETTUCCINE

- 2 pounds spinach fettuccine
- 1 cup plain yogurt
- 1 cup milk
- 2 shallots, chopped
- 1 ½ cup cream cheese
- 1 ½ cup crumbled blue cheese
- 1 cup grated Parmesan cheese
- 4 tablespoons EACH finely chopped fresh basil, marjoram and chives
- pepper

Cook fettuccine according to package directions. Drain well and return to pot. While pasta is cooking combine yogurt, milk, and shallots and simmer 3 minutes stirring occasionally. Add cheeses and stir over low heat until mixture fairly smooth. Pour over drained pasta and add herbs. Toss continuously over low heat so pasta will absorb some of the sauce. Add pepper to taste and serve immediately. 4-6 servings

TOMATO PIE

- 1 (9-inch) deep dish frozen piecrust
- 6 ounces shredded Swiss cheese
- Dijon mustard
- l large tomato, sliced ¼-inch thick
- Dried Italian herbs

Pre-heat oven to 450 degrees. Place piecrust in glass pie pan, prick bottom with fork and bake for 5-6 minutes. Reduce oven heat to 350 degrees. Spread crust with Dijon mustard. Spread Swiss cheese over mustard and top with tomato slices, tightly packed and overlapping to cover cheese. Sprinkle with dried Italian herbs and bake about 35 minutes. Let sit 10-15 minutes before cutting. Serve warm or at room temperature. 6 servings

TUNA NOODLE CASSEROLE

- 6 ounces egg noodles cooked and drained
- 1 cup mayonnaise
- 1 cup sour cream
- ½ cup grated Parmesan cheese
- ½ cup milk
- 1 teaspoon Dijon mustard
- 12 ounces tuna
- ⅓ cup chopped red pepper or pimiento
- ¼ cup (or more) chopped green onion
- 1 small (4-ounces) can chopped mushrooms, drained
- salt and pepper to taste

Pre-heat oven to 350 degrees. Cook noodles according to package directions; drain. Meanwhile in a large bowl stir together mayonnaise, sour cream, Parmesan cheese, milk and mustard. Salt and pepper to taste. Add hot noodles, tuna, red pepper, green onion and mushrooms. Stir until evenly blended. Place mixture in 2-quart baking dish. Cover and bake about 40 minutes or until hot and bubbly. 4-6 servings

TURKEY LOAF

- 1 teaspoon chicken bouillon granules
- ¼ cup boiling water
- 1 egg, slightly beaten, or ¼ cup egg substitute
- 3 slices whole wheat bread, cubed
- ¼ cup chopped onion
- ½ teaspoon dried whole sage
- ¼ teaspoon salt
- pepper to taste
- 1 pound ground turkey
- 3 tablespoons chili sauce

Pre-heat oven to 350 degrees. Dissolve bouillon granules in boiling water. Combine bouillon, egg and remaining ingredients, mixing well. Shape mixture into a 6-inch loaf, and place on rack of a lightly greased broiler pan. Bake for 55-60 minutes. 4-6 servings

TURKEY TETRAZZINI

- 1 (12-ounce) package egg noodles
- 1 (10 ¾-ounce) can cream of mushroom soup
- ½ cup milk
- ½ cup water
- 2 cups shredded cheddar cheese
- 1 ½ to 2 cups turkey, cooked and cubed
- 1 ½ cups mixed frozen peas and carrots, thawed
- 2 tablespoons pimiento
- ¼ cup seasoned breadcrumbs
- 2 tablespoons Parmesan cheese
- 2 tablespoons snipped fresh parsley (or dried)

Pre-heat oven to 375 degrees. Cook noodles according to package directions and drain. Combine soup, milk, water and cheddar cheese in 3-quart saucepan. Cook and stir over medium heat until cheese melts and sauce is hot. Stir in cooked noodles, turkey, peas, carrots and pimiento. Spoon mixture into greased 7 ½ x 11 ¾-inch baking dish. Combine crumbs, Parmesan cheese and parsley. Sprinkle over the top. Bake, uncovered, for 30 minutes or until thoroughly heated. 6 servings

UNSTUFFED CABBAGE

- 1 pound ground beef, chuck, or sirloin (I use sirloin)
- 1 cup chopped onion
- 1 small head cabbage, shred (about 1 pound)
- 1 (28-ounces) can Mexican-style tomatoes with liquid
- 1 tablespoon brown sugar
- 1 tablespoon vinegar
- ¼ teaspoon salt
- ⅛ teaspoon pepper
- hot rice

In a Dutch oven, brown beef and onion. Drain off fat. Stir in cabbage. Cover and cook for 5 minutes or until tender-crisp. Stir in tomatoes, brown sugar, vinegar, salt and pepper. Cook 10 minutes longer, stirring occasionally. Serve over hot rice. 4-6 servings

VEAL CUTLETS CORDON BLEU

- 4 (4-ounce) veal cutlets
- 4 slices Swiss cheese
- 4 (1-ounce each) slices ham
- salt and pepper
- egg wash (1 egg beaten slightly with 1 tablespoon water)
- Italian breadcrumbs
- butter

Pound veal cutlets very thin. On one half of each cutlet place a slice of Swiss cheese and slice of ham. Fold over the other side of cutlet to cover. Pound together to seal edges. Season with salt and pepper, dip in egg wash and roll in crumbs. Pan fry in butter until done, about 20 minutes. 4 servings

81

VEGETABLE PASTA

- 1 pound spaghetti
- 2 garlic cloves, crush
- ⅓ cup olive oil
- ¼ teaspoon crushed dried red pepper
- 1 bunch fresh broccoli, trimmed and cut into 1-inch pieces (may use stems, peeled and chopped)
- 1 medium tomato, cored and chopped (about 1 cup)
- 1 red or green bell pepper cut into ½-inch strips
- fresh grated Parmesan

Bring a large pot of salted water to boil. Add the broccoli and cook about 3 to 4 minutes. Then add the spaghetti and cook until the spaghetti is *al dente* and the broccoli tender (about 7 minutes more). Drain and keep warm. Heat the olive oil in a medium skillet; add garlic and dried red pepper; sauté one minute. Stir in the tomato and bell pepper and sauté about 5 minutes. Toss sauce with spaghetti and broccoli. Serve with fresh grated Parmesan. 4 servings

VEGGIE LASAGNE

- 9 lasagne noodles
- 1 (8-ounce) can tomato sauce
- 1 clove garlic, minced
- 1 teaspoon fresh chopped oregano or ¼ teaspoon dried
- 1 (10-ounce) package frozen chopped broccoli, thawed and excess liquid squeezed out
- 1 cup shredded carrot
- 1 (15 or 16-ounce) container ricotta cheese
- ¼ cup grated Parmesan cheese (fresh grated, please)
- 1 cup shredded mozzarella cheese

Pre-heat oven to 350 degrees. Cook lasagne noodles for slightly less time than the package directions indicate. In a small bowl combine tomato sauce, garlic and oregano. Mix well. In a medium bowl combine broccoli, carrot, ricotta and Parmesan. Mix well. Spray a 9 x 13-inch baking dish with vegetable cooking spray. Drain noodles. Spread ½ cup of tomato sauce over broccoli and cover with 3 more noodles cut to fit diagonally in pan. Spread with remaining broccoli mixture; top with ½ cup tomato sauce; sprinkle mozzarella over the top. Bake until bubbling, about 45 minutes. Cut into squares. You will find lasagne will be easier to slice by having alternated noodle direction. 8 servings

ZESTY PORK BAKE

- 2 tablespoons butter, melted (or use cooking spray)
- 6 rib pork chops
- salt and pepper to taste
- 1 (⅜-ounce) package dry onion soup mix
- 1 large green pepper, chopped
- 1 cup uncooked regular white rice
- ½ cup catsup
- 1 teaspoon (liberal) Worcestershire sauce
- 2 cups boiling water
- 1 cup (¼ pound) shredded cheddar cheese

Pre-heat oven to 350 degrees. Coat a shallow 2-quart casserole with the melted butter or cooking spray. Sprinkle chops with salt and pepper and arrange in casserole; top with soup mix, green pepper and rice. Combine catsup and Worcestershire sauce and spread over rice. (The dish may be prepared to this point then refrigerated until ready to bake.) Pour in boiling water, cover and bake for 55-60 minutes or until chops are done. (Additional ½ cup water may be added if casserole becomes too dry.) Remove from oven and top with shredded cheese. Cover, and allow to stand 10 minutes. 6 servings

ZUCCHINI SQUARES

- 1 cup biscuit mix
- 4 eggs, beaten
- ½ cup vegetable oil
- ½ cup grated Parmesan cheese
- ½ cup chopped onion
- 2 tablespoons chopped fresh parsley
- 1 clove garlic, minced
- ½ teaspoon seasoning salt
- ½ teaspoon dried oregano
- dash of pepper
- 2 medium zucchini, thinly sliced

Pre-heat oven to 350 degrees. Combine all ingredients except zucchini; beat well. Stir in zucchini and pour mixture into a greased 13 x 9 x 2-inch baking pan. Bake for 35 minutes or until golden brown. Let stand 10 minutes before serving. 12 squares

SALADS

APPLE-BEET SALAD

- 2 cups shredded apple
- 1 (15-ounce) can whole beets, drained and shredded
- 1 tablespoon lemon juice
- 1 tablespoon honey
- lettuce leaves
- 2 tablespoons chopped walnuts, toasted

Combine apple, beets, lemon juice, honey, tossing gently. Serve on lettuce leaves. Sprinkle with chopped walnuts. 4-6 servings

APPLESAUCE SALAD

- 3 tablespoons red cinnamon candies
- 1 cup boiling water
- 1 package orange Jell-O
- 8-ounces applesauce

Dissolve candies in boiling water. Dissolve Jell-O in hot mixture. Cool. Fold in applesauce. Pour into 4 ½ cup salad molds. Chill in refrigerate until firm. Serve on crisp greens. 4 servings

BEURY TOMATO ASPIC

- 1 quart V-8 juice (no substitute please)
- 1 (6-ounce) package lemon Jello-O
- 1 (8-ounce) package cream cheese
- juice from jar of salad olives
- mayonnaise

Dissolve Jell-O in V-8 juice over low heat. Pour half of the mixture into a greased mold (I usually use a nonstick loaf pan, but a fancy salad mold is nice if you are going to serve it whole). Chill until firm. Mix cream cheese with olive juice and mayonnaise until it is a spreading consistency. Spread over chilled layer; then pour the other half of V-8 mixture. Chill aspic until firm. Serve sliced on lettuce with a dab of mayo on top. 6-8 servings

BROCCOLI RAISIN SALAD

- 4 cups broccoli florets
- ¾ cup coarsely chopped walnuts
- ½ cup raisins
- ½ cup golden raisins
- 1 cup mayonnaise or salad dressing
- ¼ cup sugar
- 2 tablespoons lemon juice
- 2 tablespoons half-and-half
- 1 tablespoon vinegar

In a large salad bowl, toss broccoli, walnuts and raisins. In a small bowl,combine the remaining ingredients. Pour over salad; toss to coat. Cover and refrigerate for one hour before serving. 8 servings

BROCCOLI SALAD

- 1 bunch fresh broccoli, chopped
- 1 medium onion, chopped
- ½ cup chopped pecans
- 6 (or more, if small) strips of bacon, fried crisp and crumbled (may use prepared crumbled bacon)
- ½ cup raisins

Dressing:
⅔ cup mayonnaise
3 tablespoons sugar
4-5 tablespoons white vinegar

Mix dressing and pour over salad, refrigerate overnight. 4-6 servings

CHICKEN AND FRUIT SALAD

- 2 (8-ounce) cans pineapple chunks
- 1 medium apple (firm texture), diced
- 1 cup seedless grapes, halved
- 3 cups cubed cooked chicken
- 3 tablespoons butter
- 3 tablespoons all-purpose flour
- ¼ cup sugar
- 1 teaspoon salt
- ½ cup lemon juice
- 2 egg yolks, lightly beaten
- ½ cup whipping cream
- ½ slivered almonds, toasted
- lettuce leaves

Drain pineapple, reserving the juice. Set aside pineapple and ½ cup juice separately. Toss remaining juice with apple; drain. Combine chicken, pineapple, apple and grapes in a large bowl. Cover and re-frigerate. Melt butter in a saucepan and stir in flour, sugar and salt until smooth; gradually add lemon juice and reserved pineapple juice. Bring to a boil and boil for 2 minutes. Reduce heat. Add a small amount of dressing to the beaten egg yolks, then return all to the pan. Bring to another gentle boil; cook and stir for 2 minutes. Remove from heat and chill for 10-15 minutes. Beat cream until it forms stiff peaks; fold into cooled dressing. Pour over chicken mixture; gently stir to coat. Chill for 1 hour and serve on lettuce with sprinkle of toasted slivered almonds. 6-8 servings

CHICKEN SALAD

- 2 cups chopped cooked chicken
- 1 cup chopped celery
- 1 cup seedless grapes, cut in half
- ½ cup chopped almonds, toasted
- 1 (11-ounce) can mandarin oranges, drained
- ½ cup mayonnaise
- 1 teaspoon grated onion
- ¼ teaspoon salt
- lettuce leaves

Combine chicken, celery and next 3 ingredients in a bowl. Combine mayonnaise, onion, salt and add to chicken mixture, stirring gently. Serve on lettuce leaves. 4-8 servings

COLESLAW

- 1 Granny Smith apple, coarsely shredded
- ½ medium green cabbage, halved lengthwise and sliced very thin
- (about 4 cups)
- ½ medium red cabbage, halved lengthwise and sliced very thin
- (about 4 cups)
- 2 carrots, finely shredded

Dressing:
- ½ cup mayonnaise
- 1 tablespoon honey
- 2 teaspoons cider vinegar
- ½ teaspoon salt

In a large bowl whisk together dressing ingredients. Add apple, cabbages, carrots. Toss well and chill until serving. 6-8 servings

CORN BREAD SALAD

- 1 (6-ounce) package Mexican corn bread mix
- 1 (4.5-ounce) can diced green chilies
- 1 cup chopped green bell pepper
- 3 large tomatoes, chopped
- 2 (16-ounce) cans pinto beans, drained
- 2 (16 ¼-ounce) cans whole kernal corn, drained
- 1 cup sliced green onions (tops and some bulbs)
- 1 (16-ounce) bottle Ranch dressing (I used Kraft Light Done Right)
- 1 (8-ounce) package shredded Cheddar cheese
- ½ to 1 cup real bacon bits (may use imitation, if desired)
- shredded letuce

Prepare corn bread mix according to package directions, adding green chilies; bake as directed and cool. Combine green peppers, tomatoes, corn, green onions, dressing, cheese and bacon. Crumble half of the corn bread into a bowl and top with mixed ingredients. Repeat layers. Cover salad and chill for at least two hours before serving. Serve over shredded lettuce. 8 large servings

CREAMY TOMATO SALAD

- 1 large tomato, chopped
- 1 large cucumber, peeled
- 1 small red onion, thinly sliced
- 1 cup (8-ounces) sour cream
- 1 tablespoon sugar
- 1 tablespoon white vinegar
- salt and pepper to taste
- leaf lettuce (optional)

In a bowl, combine tomato, cucumber and onion. In another bowl, combine sour cream, sugar, vinegar, salt and pepper; mix well. Pour over vegetables and toss to coat. Refrigerate until serving. Serve over lettuce, if desired. 6 servings

CURRIED BROCCOLI SALAD

- 1 ½ pounds fresh broccoli
- 1 cup sour cream
- ¼ cup milk
- ½ teaspoon curry powder
- ¼ teaspoon seasoned salt
- ¼ teaspoon dry mustard
- pepper to taste

Discard tough ends of stalks and cut florets and small stems into bite-size pieces. Steam broccoli 8-10 minutes until crisp-tender. Cool. Combine remaining ingredients in a small bowl. Pour over broccoli and gently toss to coat. Cover and cool 2-3 hours before serving. 4-6 servings

CURRIED CHICKEN SALAD

- 2 cups chopped chicken
- 3 hard boiled eggs, chopped
- 3 stalks celery, chopped
- 1 medium onion, chopped
- 1 cup (or more if needed) mayonnaise
- 2 teaspoons curry powder

Mix mayonnaise and curry powder. Add to chopped ingredients and mix well. Chill before serving. makes 1 quart

CURRIED RICE SALAD

- 1 cup rice (I use Jasmine)
- 1 tablespoon of curry powder
- ½ of an 11-ounce can Mandarin oranges
- 1 Red Delicious apple with peeling, chopped

- 1 cup diced celery
- ½ cup pineapple pieces
- ½ cup white raisins
- ½ cup slivered almonds
- 4 green onions, chopped

Beau dressing:
- 2 tablespoons sugar*
- 1 teaspoon salt
- ½ teaspoon pepper
- 2 ounces vegetable oil

- 3 tablespoons rice wine (or regular) vinegar
- 3 drops Sesame seed oil

*If using regular vinegar use 3 tablespoons sugar

Mix all ingredients well. May double recipe and use as dressing for any green salad.

Add curry powder to water in which rice is cooked according to package directions. Add raisins to rice while still warm. Then add remaining ingredients and mix with Beau dressing. Chill before serving. May add chicken or ham. 6-8 servings

FROZEN FRUIT SALAD

- 1 envelope unflavored gelatin
- ¼ cup cold water
- 2 cups canned fruit cocktail with syrup
- ½ cup mayonnaise
- 1 cup heavy cream, whipped
- ⅓ cup Maraschino cherries

Soften gelatin in cold water, dissolve over hot water and cool slightly. Add fruit cocktail with syrup. Fold in mayonnaise and whipped cream. Pour into a refrigerator tray and dot with cherries. Freeze until just firm. 6 servings

FRUIT SALAD

- 2 cups diced pineapple
- 2 apples, diced and sprinkled with lemon juice
- 2 oranges, peeled and sliced
- 2 bananas, sliced and sprinkled with lemon juice
- 1 cup halved seedless green or red grapes
- ½ cup chopped celery
- ½ cup dry roasted peanuts
- ½ cup raisins
- 4-6 ounces shredded Cheddar cheese

Dressing: l cup plain yogurt mixed with ⅓ cup honey

Gently toss all ingredients, except cheese, together. Chill. Sprinkle with cheese and top with dressing before serving. 6-8 servings

GREENBRIER CHICKEN SALAD

- 2 ½ pound chicken
- 1 cup diced celery (3 medium ribs)
- ⅔ cup sour cream
- 1 ⅓ cup mayonnaise
- 2 tablespoons white wine vinegar
- salt and freshly ground black pepper, to taste

Put the chicken in a large stock pot with lightly salted cold water to cover. Bring to boil, reduce heat to simmer and poach gently, skimming off any foam accumulating on the surface. Simmer until the meat is very tender when pierced with a knife, 50-60 minutes. Leave chicken to cool in poaching water. When cooled enough to handle, remove all the meat, discarding any skin, fat. Cut the meat into ½-inch pieces. The chicken may be prepared up to one day ahead and the chicken stock may be frozen and saved for another recipe. Mix together the diced chicken, diced celery, sour cream, mayonnaise and vinegar. Season to taste with salt and pepper. Chill well before serving. 6-8 servings

GREENS AND CRANBERRY SALAD

- 6 cups torn iceberg lettuce
- 6 cups torn romaine
- 3 green onions, thinly sliced
- 1 celery stalk, thinly sliced
- ¼ cup vegetable oil
- ¼ cup white vinegar
- ¼ cup sugar
- 1 tablespoon minced fresh parsley
- ½ to 1 teaspoon hot pepper sauce
- ¾ cup to 1 cup dried cranberries
- ¼ cup sliced almonds, toasted

In a large bowl, combine greens, onions and celery. In a small bowl, combine oil, vinegar, sugar, parsley, hot pepper sauce and salt; mix well. Pour over salad and toss to coat. Add cranberries and almonds. Serve immediately. 10-12 servings

GRILLED CHICKEN AND PASTA SALAD

- 1 ½ cups Italian salad dressing
- ½ cup cider vinegar
- ⅓ cup honey
- 2 teaspoons dried oregano
- 1 teaspoon dried basil
- ½ teaspoon pepper
- 6 boneless, skinless chicken breasts (1 ½ pounds)
- 1 (12-ounce) package fettuccine
- 1 ½ cups broccoli florets
- 3 medium carrots, thinly sliced
- 2 ribs of celery, thinly sliced
- 1 cup green pepper, chopped
- ½ cup (or more, if desired) sliced ripe olives (may use canned, drain)

Dressing:
- 1 ½ cups Italian salad dressing
- 1 teaspoon garlic salt
- 1 teaspoon dried oregano
- 1 teaspoon Italian seasoning

In a large sealable plastic bag or shallow glass container, combine first six ingredients. Cut chicken breasts into strips and add to marinate mixture. Seal or cover and refrigerate for 2-3 hours. While chicken is marinating, cook fettuccine according to package directions; drain and cool. Also make dressing and put in jar with lid. Drain and discard marinade. Grill chicken, uncovered, over medium heat for 4-5 minutes on each side, until juices run clear. Cut into bite-sized pieces or small strips; set aside. Combine vegetables, olives and fettuccine in a large bowl. Shake dressing well and pour over salad; toss to coat. Top with chicken. 6 servings

HOMESTEAD SALAD

- 1 (10-ounce) package frozen mixed vegetables
- 1 (16-ounce) can red kidney beans, drained
- ½ cup chopped green pepper
- ½ cup diced onion
- 1 cup diced celery
- 1 tablespoon all-purpose flour
- ¾ cup sugar
- 1 tablespoon prepared mustard
- ½ cup white vinegar

Cook mixed vegetables according to package directions, drain. Set aside to cool. Rinse kidney beans and drain well. Combine celery, onion, green pepper, mixed vegetables and kidney beans. Combine flour, sugar, mustard and vinegar. Cook over medium heat, stirring constantly, until clear and thick. Let cool; then stir into vegetable mixture. Refrigerate for 24 hours, stirring occasionally. 6-8 servings

ITALIAN PASTA SALAD

- ½ cup mayonnaise
- 1 tablespoon red wine vinegar
- 1 teaspoon salt
- ¼ teaspoon pepper
- ¼ teaspoon cayenne pepper (optional)
- 1 clove garlic, minced
- 1 ½ tablespoons fresh chopped basil
- 2 cups colored corkscrew pasta
- 1 cup chopped tomatoes
- ½ cup chopped yellow bell pepper
- ½ cup sliced black olives
- ¼ cup jarred roasted red peppers
- ½ cup chopped salami
- ¼ cup Feta cheese (or more to taste)

Cook pasta according to package directions, rinse with cold water and drain. Whisk together mayonnaise, vinegar, salt, peppers, and garlic. Mix in basil. Combine pasta, vegetables, olives and salami. Fold in dressing and mix well. Chill several hours. Before serving add Feta cheese and mix gently. 6-8 servings

JELLIED BROCCOLI SALAD

- 2 (10-ounce) packages broccoli (or 1 fresh head)
- 1 (10 ¾ ounce) can beef consomme
- 1 ½ envelopes plain gelatine
- 6 hard boiled eggs, chopped fine
- 1 cup mayonnaise
- salt and pepper to taste

Cook, drain, cool and chop broccoli very fine. Dissolve gelatine in ½ can cold consomme. Heat other ½ of consomme and mix with cold. Add broccoli and eggs to consomme. Let cool to room temperature, then add mayonnaise. Season to taste with salt and pepper. Put into salad molds and chill until serving. 8-10 servings

LAYERED LETTUCE SALAD

- 1 solid head of lettuce, shredded
- 1 package (10-ounce) frozen peas
- 1 package cauliflower florets, cut small
- 1 red onion, chopped
- 1 package shredded sharp cheddar cheese
- 1 package crumbled real bacon bits

Dressing:
- 2 cups mayonnaise
- ⅓ cup Parmesan cheese
- 1 teaspoon salt
- pepper to taste
- ¼ cup sugar

Make layers (two) with all ingredients, using as much cheese and bacon bits as desired. Mix dressing well in a small bowl. Spread dressing over salad to seal. Cover and refrigerate overnight. Toss well before serving. 8-10 servings

LAYERED PASTA SALAD

- 1½ cups medium-sized macaroni shells, cooked, rinsed with cold water, drained
- 1 tablespoon vegetable oil

Dressing:
- 1 cup mayonnaise
- ½ cup sour cream
- 2 teaspoons Dijon mustard
- ¼ cup sliced green onions
- ½ teaspoon salt
- ½ teaspoon freshly ground pepper
- 2 cups shredded iceberg lettuce (may substitute fresh spinach or other types of lettuce)
- 3 hard-cooked eggs, sliced
- pepper to taste
- 12-ounces ham, cut in thin strips
- 1 (10-ounce) package frozen tiny peas, thawed
- 1 cup coarsely shredded Monterey Jack cheese

Toss macaroni with oil to prevent shells from sticking together. Mix all dressing ingredients until thoroughly blended. Put lettuce in one layer of a 3-quart bowl; top with the cooled macaroni, then egg slices. Sprinkle with pepper. Add in layers the ham, peas and cheese. Spread dressing over the top to the bowls edge. Cover tightly plastic wrap and refrigerate overnight. Before serving, sprinkle with chopped fresh parsley. For a more dramatic presentation, use a glass or clear plastic bowl to show off the layers and toss at the table. 6 servings

LAYERED SPINACH SALAD

- 1 shaker of grated Romano/Parmesan cheese
- 1 package crumbled real bacon bit
- 6 (10-ounce) baby spinach (about 1 ½ quart)
- 6-8 large mushrooms (about 2 cups) sliced
- 1 medium (about 1 cup) red onion, sliced into rings
- 1 package (10-ounce) frozen peas

Dressing:
- ½ cup mayonnaise
- ½ cup sour cream
- 1 teaspoon sugar

Combine ½ cheese with ¼ cup bacon bits. In a large bowl layer spinach, cheese mixture, mushrooms, onions and peas (makes 2 layers) and end with spinach. Combine dressing ingredients and mix well. Spread over salad to seal. Sprinkle 2 tablespoons cheese over top. Cover and refrigerate overnight. Mix well before serving. 8-10 servings

LIMA BEAN SALAD

- 2 (10-ounce) packages frozen lima beans
- 2 (10-ounce) packages frozen green beans
- 2 (10-ounce) packages frozen green peas
- 6 hard-cooked eggs, chopped
- 1 small onion, grated
- 1 cup mayonnaise
- 2 teaspoons prepared mustard
- 4 teaspoons salad oil
- 4 tablespoons olive oil (virgin cold pressed is best)
- dash (or more, if desired) Tabasco sauce and Worcestershire sauce

Cook and drain beans and peas according to package directions. Fold in eggs and onion. Mix mayonnaise, mustard, salad oil, olive oil, Tabasco and Worcestershire. Mix with salad ingredients and let stand overnight in refrigerator. 8-10 servings

Salads

MACARONI AND VEGGIE SALAD

- 1 (12-ounce) package multi-colored (garden) spiral pasta
- 1 green pepper, chopped
- 1 cucumber, chopped
- 1 carrot shaved
- ½ large red onion, chopped
- 2 tablespoons (or more) mayonnaise
- 2 tablespoons (or more) ranch (may use light) dressing
- Salad Supreme seasoning

Cook pasta according to package directions, rinse in cold water and drain. Prepare vegetables and mix well with Salad Supreme seasoning to taste. Mix mayonnaise and ranch dressing and add to pasta/vegetable mixture until well coated. Adjust seasoning. 6-8 servings

MACARONI SALAD

- ¾ cup mayonnaise
- 2 tablespoons cider vinegar
- 1 tablespoon prepared mustard
- 1 teaspoon sugar
- 1 teaspoon salt
- ¼ teaspoon pepper
- 8 ounces elbow macaroni cooked according to package rinsed with cold water and drained
- 1 cup diced celery
- 1 cup chopped green (or red) pepper
- 5 chopped green onions (with some green) or ¼ cup chopped onion

In a large bowl combine first 5 ingredients. Add remaining ingredients and toss to mix. Cover and chill several hours before serving. 8-10 servings

MARIE'S MAC SALAD

- 1 pound corkscrew macaroni or about 1½ pounds elbow macaroni
- 1 medium purple onion, diced
- 1 to 2 cucumbers, diced
- 3 medium tomatoes, diced
- 1 bunch green onion, sliced (bulbs and stems)
- 1 ½ pound jar of Kroger dill pickles, diced
- 1 green pepper, diced
- 1 small package radishes, thinly sliced
- 3 hard-cooked eggs, diced
- 1 shaved carrot (mainly for color but may add more)
- 1 quart jar of Kraft Real Mayonnaise
- salt and pepper to taste

Cook macaroni according to package directions. Add all ingredients. Add mayonnaise to taste , salt, pepper, and mix well. Cover and chill at least 8 hours before serving. 6-8 servings

Note: Use as much, or as little, of the vegetable you like, or add others. For example, in the summer, when the price is lower, use a red or yellow pepper instead of the green.

MOCK CRAB SALAD

- 1 cup orzo pasta
- 1 clove garlic
- ½ pound plum tomatoes, peeled and diced
- 1 (2 ¼-ounce) can pitted black olives, sliced
- ¼ cup red onion, chopped
- ⅓ cup red bell pepper, diced
- ½ cup cumcumber, peeled and diced
- 1 pound mock crab meat, cut into small chunks
- 2 tablespoons Zesty Italian Salad Dressing
- ¼ teaspoon pepper

Put garlic clove in water and cook orzo according to package directions. Discard garlic when draining. Mix all remaining ingredients and chill at least 4 hours before serving. 4-6 servings

ORANGE FLUFF SALAD

- 1 (16-ounce) can sliced peaches
- 1 (15-20-ounce) can pineapple tidbits
- 2 Red Delicious apples
- 2 bananas
- 1 (11-ounce) can Mandarin oranges
- 1 carton plain yogurt (or may use lemon or pineapple)
- 1 (3-ounce) package instant vanilla pudding
- ⅓ cup orange juice
- 1 ½ cup milk

Cut all fruit into bite-size pieces. Mix pudding, milk and orange juice. Beat in yogurt. Toss with fruit and refrigerate at least two hours before serving. 6-8 servings

RED AND WHITE BEAN SALAD

- 2 cans (15-ounces each) red kidney beans, drained
- 2 cans (15-ounce each) white kidney beans, drained
- 2 small onions, thinly sliced
- ½ cup diced celery
- ⅓ cup vegetable oil
- ½ cup cider vinegar
- ½ teaspoon dry mustard
- ½ teaspoon garlic salt
- ¼ teaspoon pepper

Combine beans, onions, and celery in a large bowl. Combine remaining ingredients in a small bowl and blend thoroughly. Pour dressing over bean salad, toss lightly. Cover and chill thoroughly before serving. 8-10 servings

REFRIGERATOR CUCUMBERS

- 1 (16-ounce) can sliced peaches
- 7 cups of thinly sliced cucumbers
- 1 large onion thinly sliced
- 1 teaspoon celery seed
- 1 cup white vinegar
- 2 cups sugar

Slice cucumbers and onion and put in sealable container. Mix other ingredients and pour over vegetables. Put container in refrigerator to chill for several hours before serving. Keeps several weeks in refrigerator.

RIPE OLIVE POTATO SALAD

- 2 cups diced cooked potatoes
- 3 tablespoons olive oil
- 1 tablespoon white vinegar
- 1 ½ teaspoon salt
- ⅛ teaspoon pepper
- ½ cup ripe (black) olives
- 2 hard boiled eggs
- 1 cup diced celery
- ¼ cup diced dill pickle
- ¼ cup sliced pimientos
- ⅓ cup mayonnaise
- 1 teaspoon grated onion

Blend olive oil, vinegar and salt and pepper. Pour over potatoes and mix. Cut olives into large pieces, dice eggs and add with celery, dill pickle and pimientos to other ingredients. Then add mayonnaise and grated onion. Mix well and chill in refrigerator. 4-6 servings

SEA FOOD PASTA SALAD

- 3 cups corkscrew pasta, cooked and drained
- ½ pound cooked shrimp
- 1 (6-ounce) can crab meat, drained, flaked
- 1 cup broccoli florets, partially cooked
- 1 cup chopped green pepper
- 2 small tomatoes, cut into wedges
- ¼ cup green onions, chopped
- ½ cup salad dressing
- ¼ cup grated Parmesan cheese
- 1 (8-ounce) bottle Italian dressing

In a large bowl combine pasta, shrimp, crab, vegetables and mix lightly. Combine salad dressing, Parmesan cheese and gradually add Italian dressing, mixing until blended. Add to pasta mix and chill overnight (or at least 4 hours) before serving. 6-8 servings

SHRIMP AND RICE SALAD

- 3 tablespoons soy sauce, divided
- 1 cup uncooked long grain rice
- ½ pound cooked baby shrimp
- 1 carrot, peeled and shredded
- ½ cup frozen green peas, thawed and drained
- ½ cup chopped green onions with tops
- 1 tablespoon minced fresh ginger root
- ¼ cup distilled white vinegar
- 2 tablespoons sugar
- 2 teaspoons toasted sesame seeds

Combine 2 tablespoons soy sauce and 2 cups of water in medium sauce pan. Bring to boil; stir in rice. Reduce heat and simmer, covered, 20 minutes or until water is absorbed. Remove from heat and cool. Rinse shrimp, drain thoroughly. Reserve ½ cup of shrimp. Combine remaining shrimp, carrot, peas, green onions and ginger root in a large bowl. Fluff rice with fork; fold into shrimp mixture. Cover and refrigerate until chilled. Measure vinegar, sugar, remaining soy sauce, sesame seed and 2 teaspoons water into a cruet or screw-top jar with lid. Shake until blended and sugar dissolves. When ready to serve salad, pour dressing over rice mixture and toss and coat all ingredients well. Sprinkle each serving with reserved shrimp. 4 servings

SHRIMP SALAD

- 1 pound boiled shrimp, peeled and deveined
- ¼ cup minced celery
- 2 tablespoons minced onion
- 1 ¼ cup shrimp sauce
- 1 head iceberg lettuce, shredded
- 3-6 tomatoes, cut into wedges
- Garnish: chopped fresh chives

Shrimp Sauce:
- 2 cups mayonnaise
- 6 tablespoons catsup
- 4 teaspoons mustard
- 4 teaspoons lemon juice
- 2 teaspoons Worcestershire sauce
- 1 teaspoon garlic powder

Mix all ingredients well.

Coarsely chop shrimp and place in a bowl. Stir celery, onion and shrimp sauce. Add shrimp and toss. Serve over iceberg lettuce with tomato wedges. Garnish, if desired. Makes about 2 ½ cups

SHRIMP-TUNA-MACARONI SALAD

- 2 cups cooked macaroni
- 1 ½ cups chopped celery
- 1 (5-ounce) can tuna
- 1 package frozen salad shrimp (shelled, deveined, cooked) thawed
- ¼ - ½ cup sliced green olives
- ½ medium green (or red) pepper
- 4 green onions (bulb and stem) chopped
- 1 cup mayonnaise
- ¼ tablespoon black pepper
- salt to taste

Cook macaroni according to package directions, rinse in cold water and drain. Combine macaroni with next 6 ingredients and mix well. Combine mayonnaise, pepper and salt, mix well. Add dressing to salad and mix until well coated. Chill before serving. 6-8 servings

SOUR CREAM POTATO SALAD

- 3 pounds new or regular potatoes, cooked and cubed
  (I usually use new and leave the skins on)
- 1 cup (or more) diced celery
- 1 green pepper, diced
- 2 bunches of green onions with some stem, chopped or 6-10
  ramps (bulb only), chopped
- 5 or 6 radishes, chopped (optional)

Dressing:
- 1 cup sour cream (or plain yogurt)
- 1 cup mayonnaise
- 2 teaspoons seasoned salt
- 2 teaspoons dill weed
- generous dash of fresh ground pepper and garlic powder
  (omit if using ramps)

Mix dressing well in a separate bowl, then toss lightly with potato mixture. Chill at least 4 hours before serving. 8 servings

SWEET AND SOUR CUCUMBERS

- 2 medium cucumbers
- 3 medium onions
- ½ cup white vinegar
- ½ cup sugar
- ½ teaspoon salt

Do not peel cucumbers; score lengthwise with tines of fork and slice paper-thin. Slice onions, separate into rings; combine with cucumbers. Combine vinegar, sugar, salt; stir over low heat until sugar dissolves; bring to a boil, pour over cucumbers and onions. Chill. 6-8 servings

TOMATO/BREAD SALAD

- ¼ cup red wine vinegar
- 1 tablespoon Dijon mustard
- 2 cloves of garlic, minced
- ½ teaspoon salt
- ½ teaspoon pepper
- ⅔ cup olive oil
- 6 cups French bread cubes
  (choose day-old, crusty French for right texture)
- 5 cups seeded, diced tomatoes
- 2 large cucumbers, peeled, seeded and diced
- ½ cup chopped purple onion
- ½ cup shaved Parmesan cheese
- 1 cup thinly sliced basil leaves

In a large bowl whisk together first five ingredients then whisk in olive oil in a slow, steady stream until well blended. Stir in bread cubes and next five ingredients. Let salad stand at least 5 minutes before serving. 4-6 servings

TOMATO SALAD

- 4 tomatoes, cut into bite-size pieces
- 1 cucumber, thinly sliced
- ¾ to 1 cup chopped purple onion
- 2 teaspoons dried whole oregano
- 1 teaspoon dried whole basil
- ½ teaspoon salt
- ⅔ cup crumbled Feta cheese
- ½ cup olive oil

Combine first 3 ingredients in a bowl; sprinkle with herbs and salt. Cover and chill at least 1 hour. Add Feta cheese and olive oil and toss lightly before serving. 4-6 servings

TUNA PASTA SALAD

- 2 cups cooked and chilled penne pasta
- 2 cups frozen broccoli, cauliflower and red pepper mix, steamed and chilled
- ½ cup chopped fresh basil or 2 tablespoons dried
- ¼ cup sliced black olives
- 2 tablespoons minced green onions, including tops
- 12 ounces tuna, drained and chunked
- 1 cup creamy Italian salad dressing or bottled Alfredo sauce
- 3 cups mixed salad greens
- ½ cup grated Parmesan or Romano cheese

In a large bowl, combine all ingredients except greens and cheese. Chill 2-3 hours. Divide salad greens for each portion and spoon generously with tuna mixture. Garnish with cheese. 6 servings

VEGETABLE SALAD

- ¾ cup white vinegar
- ½ cup vegetable oil
- 1 cup sugar
- 1 teaspoon salt
- 1 teaspoon pepper
- 2 (11-ounce) cans white corn, drained
- 1 (15 ounce) can small sweet peas, drained
- 1 (14 ½ ounce) can French-style green beans, drained
- 1 cup diced green pepper
- 1 cup diced celery
- l cup chopped onion
- ¼ cup diced pimientos, drained

Bring first 5 ingredients to a boil in a small saucepan over medium-high heat, stirring until sugar dissolves. Cool. Combine corn and next 6 ingredients in a bowl; stir in vinegar mixture. Mix. Chill 8 hours; drain before serving. 10-12 servings

VIDALIA ONION & BERRY SALAD

- 8 cups torn Bibb lettuce
- 1 pint fresh strawberries, cut in half
- 1 cup fresh blueberries
- 1 cup fresh raspberries
- 1 Vidalia onion, halved and sliced
- sweet vidalia dressing (recipe follows)

Toss lettuce, berries and onion slices together and serve with dressing. 8 servings

Dressing:
- ¼ cup grated Vidalia onion
- ¼ cup sugar
- ⅓ cup apple cider vinegar
- ¼ cup vegetable oil
- ½ teaspoon dry mustard
- ¼ teaspoon salt
- ¼ teaspoon freshly ground
- black pepper

Combine all ingredients in a jar; cover tightly and shake vigorously. Makes one cup.

VEGETABLES
AND
SIDE DISHES

ASPARAGUS CASSEROLE

- 1 (10 ¾-ounce) can cream of mushroom soup
- 2 (15-ounce) cans asparagus
- ½ cup almonds, slivered and toasted
- ½ cup milk
- 2 eggs, beaten
- Ritz cracker crumbs

Pre-heat oven to 325 degrees. In a greased baking dish put a layer of asparagus and a layer of almonds and repeat. Mix soup, milk and eggs and pour over top of layers. Top with cracker crumbs and dot with butter. Bake until thickened for about 30 minutes. 6-8 servings

BAKED BROCCOLI

- 2 (10-ounce) packages frozen chopped broccoli, cooked according to package directions and drained
- 1 cup grated sharp cheddar cheese
- 2 eggs, beaten
- 1 cup mayonnaise
- 1 can (10 ¾-ounce) cream of mushroom soup

Pre-heat oven to 350 degrees. Mix all ingredients together and place in a lightly greased baking dish. Bake about 30-45 minutes till heated through. 6-8 servings

BAKED EGGPLANT
AND TOMATO

- 1 ½ pounds eggplant, sliced thick
- 1 clove garlic, crushed
- 1 pound ripe tomatoes, peeled and chopped
- 1 teaspoon sugar
- 5 tablespoons grated Parmesan (fresh)
- olive oil
- salt and pepper
- ¼ cup chopped fresh basil
- ½ pound mozzarella, diced

Pre-heat oven to 350 degrees. Salt the eggplant slices and leave for about 30 minutes to let the juices run out. Sauté the garlic in 2 tablespoons olive oil until soft, but not brown. Add the tomatoes, sugar, a little salt and pepper, and the basil. Cook until reduced to a thick sauce. Rinse, drain and dry the eggplant slices. Brown slices in hot olive oil, turning once. Drain on paper towels. Arrange eggplant slices in a baking dish, cover with tomato sauce, sprinkle with the mozzarella and Parmesan. Bake for about 30 minutes. 4 servings

BAKED RISOTTO

- 1 tablespoon butter
- 1 small onion, minced
- ¾ cup uncooked Arborio rice
- 14 ½ ounces chicken broth
- ½ teaspoon dried Italian seasoning
- ¼ teaspoon salt
- ¼ teaspoon pepper

Pre-heat oven to 350 degrees. Melt butter in a 10-inch ovenproof skillet over medium heat. Add onion and sauté until tender. Add rice; cook, stirring constantly, 3 minutes. Stir in broth, bring to a boil. Stir in remaining ingredients. Bake, covered for 30 minutes or until liquid absorbed. 4 servings

BAKED SPINACH CASSEROLE

- 2 (10-ounce) packages frozen chopped spinach
- 2 eggs, beaten
- 1 tablespoon flour
- ½ teaspoon salt
- ⅛ teaspoon pepper
- 2 teaspoons lemon juice
- ⅛ teaspoon (or more to taste) garlic powder

Pre-heat oven to 350 degrees. Cook spinach as directed on package, except simmer only 3 minutes. Drain. To beaten eggs add flour, seasonings, lemon juice and beat with mixer until smooth. Add cooked spinach and mix well. Place in lightly greased 1-quart casserole. Bake uncovered 20-25 minutes. 6-8 servings

BAKED STUFFED TOMATOES

- 8 large tomatoes
- ½ medium onion, chopped
- 2 tablespoons fresh Italian parsley, chopped
- 10 fresh mushrooms, diced
- 2 fresh garlic cloves, diced
- 1 pound cooked brown rice
- salt and pepper to taste
- 3 tablespoons olive oil

Pre-heat oven to 375 degrees. Slice off rounded bottoms of tomatoes, scoop out insides. Mix onion, garlic, and mushrooms with tomato pulp. Put oil in 9 x 12-inch baking dish and add tomato mixture. Bake 7 minutes. Remove from oven and pour mixture in a bowl. Blend in rice, parsley and seasonings. Stuff tomatoes with this mixture and bake for 20 minutes. 8 servings

BEANS AND GREENS

- ½ pound dry great northern, navy, pinto or kidney beans
- 1 (14.5-ounce) can chicken stock
- 1 clove garlic, minced
- ¼ teaspoon dried crushed red pepper (optional)
- 4 cups mustard greens or spinach,
- cleaned and torn into bite-size pieces
- 1 bay leaf
- 1 teaspoon dried thyme, crushed
- ¼ teaspoon salt and pepper
- 4 slices bacon
- 1 medium onion, chopped

Rinse beans. In a large saucepan combine beans and 4 cups of cold water. Bring to boiling; reduce heat. Simmer 2 minutes. Remove from heat. Cover; let stand 1 hour. Drain and rinse beans. Return beans to the saucepan and add 2 ½ cups fresh cold water, the chicken stock, bay leaf, thyme, salt and pepper. Bring to boiling; reduce heat. Cover and simmer about 1 ¼ hours or until beans are tender, stirring occasionally. Add more water during cooking if needed. Meanwhile, fry bacon, in a large skillet, until crisp. Drain, reserving 1 tablespoon of drippings in the skillet. Add onion, garlic, crushed red pepper and cook, stir over medium heat until onion tender Add greens, cover and cook 1-2 minutes. Drain beans, reserving liquid if desired. Discard bay leaf. Return beans to saucepan and add onion/greens mixture, tossing gently to combine. Season to taste with additional salt and pepper. Spoon into serving bowls and crumble bacon over top. If desired, use broth (if saved) to add to dish. 6 servings

BEEFY RICE

- 1 (6.8-ounces) package beef-flavored rice mix
- 1 pound boneless round steak, cut into ⅛-inch strips
- 1 tablespoon butter
- 2 cups broccoli florets
- 1 small onion, thinly sliced
- ½ cup julienne green or red pepper

Prepare rice according to package directions. Meanwhile, in a skillet, sauté beef in butter for 2-3 minutes. Add beef, broccoli, onion and pepper to rice. Simmer uncovered for 10 minutes or until vegetables are tender-crisp. 4 servings

BROCCOLI AND CELERY CASSEROLE

- 1 (10-ounce) package frozen chopped broccoli
  (or 1 ½ cups fresh, cooked)
- 2 cups celery cut into ½-inch slices
- ¼ cup butter
- 1 cup shredded American cheese (about ½ pound)
- ¼ teaspoon flour
- ½ teaspoon salt
- ¼ teaspoon pepper
- 2 cups milk

Pre-heat oven to 350 degrees. Cook broccoli according to package directions, drain. Cook celery in boiling salted water until crisply tender (5-6 minutes). Combine the 2 vegetables in a buttered 1 ½ quart baking dish. Melt butter in a saucepan, add flour and blend. Add milk stirring constantly and cook until sauce smooth and thickened. Add salt and pepper and mix. Pour over vegetables. Cover with cheese and bake for 15-20 minutes or until thoroughly heated. 6 servings

BROCCOLI-BLUE CHEESE CASSEROLE

- 2 tablespoons butter
- 1 tablespoon all-purpose flour
- 3 ounces cream cheese
- 1 ½ ounces blue cheese
- 1 cup milk
- 20 ounces frozen chopped broccoli, thawed and drained
- ⅓ cup cracker crumbs

Pre-heat oven to 350 degrees. Grease a shallow, 1-quart baking dish. In a saucepan over medium heat, melt the butter. Stir in the flour until blended. Stir in the cream and blue cheeses until melted. Gradually stir in the milk, simmer and stir until thickened. Add the broccoli to the sauce, stir, then transfer to the baking dish. Top with cracker crumbs and bake about 30 minutes until broccoli cooked and crumbs are light brown. 8 servings

BROCCOLI-PARMESAN GRATIN

- 1 bunch fresh broccoli (about 1 ½ pounds)
- 1 cup whole milk
- ½ cup heavy cream
- 1 cup grated Parmesan cheese (Parmigiano-Reggiano preferred)
- 2 large eggs
- 1 cup coarse fresh bread crumbs
- 1 tablespoon extra-virgin olive oil
- ½ teaspoon salt and pepper

Preheat oven to 350 degrees with rack in upper third of oven. Cut broccoli florets into 1-inch pieces, then peel large stems and cut into ½-inch thick rounds. Cook broccoli in boiling salted water for 5 minutes, then drain. Meantime, whisk together milk, cream, cheese, eggs, and salt and pepper. Put broccoli in a 2-quart shallow baking dish, then pour milk mixture over top. Toss breadcrumbs with oil and a pinch of salt and pepper, then sprinkle evenly over top. Bake until custard is set, about 30 minutes. Turn on broiler, then broil until bread crumbs are golden brown (about 2-3 minutes). Let stand 5 minutes before serving. Makes 4 main course or 6 side dishes

BROCCOLI-RICE CASSEROLE

- 1 medium onion, chopped
- ½ stick butter
- 1 package (10 or 12 ounces) chopped broccoli, cooked and drained
- 1 cup prepared rice (may use Minute)
- 1 (10 ¾-ounce) can cream of celery or cream of mushroom soup
- ¼ cup water
- ½ cup Cheez-Whiz
- ½ cup milk

Pre-heat oven to 350 degrees. Sauté onion in butter then add to other ingredients, mixing well. Pour into a greased casserole dish and bake 30-40 minutes. 4-6 servings

BRUSSELS SPROUTS AND RICE

- 1 (10 ¾-ounce) can cream of celery soup, undiluted
- 1 cup milk
- 1 cup water
- 1 tablespoon butter
- 1 teaspoon salt
- ⅔ cup uncooked rice
- 2 (10-ounce) packages frozen Brussels sprouts

Combine soup, milk, water, butter, and salt in a medium saucepan; bring to a boil. Stir in rice and cover; reduce heat and simmer mixture 15 minutes, stirring occasionally. Stir in Brussels sprouts; cover and cook 15 minutes or until sprouts are tender. 6-8 servings

CASHEW RICE PILAF

- 1 ½ cups uncooked long-grain rice
- 1 cup chopped onion
- 1 cup diced carrots
- 1 cup golden raisins
- ¼ cup butter
- 3 cups chicken stock
- 1 teaspoon onion salt
- 2 cups frozen peas
- 1 ½ cups cooked wild rice
- 1 cup cashews
- ¼ cup thinly sliced green onions

In a Dutch oven, sauté the long-grain rice, onion, carrots and raisins in butter until the onion is tender. Add the chicken stock and onion salt; bring to a boil. Reduce heat; cover and simmer for 20 minutes or until liquid is absorbed and rice is tender. Stir in peas, wild rice and cashews; heat through. Sprinkle with green onions. 12 servings

CAULIFLOWER AU GRATIN

- 1 (10-ounce) package frozen cauliflower, defrosted
- ½ cup milk
- ¼ cup water
- 1 teaspoon cornstarch
- salt and pepper to taste
- 2 tablespoons shredded extra-sharp cheddar cheese (more, if desired)
- 2 teaspoons seasoned breadcrumbs

Pre-heat oven to 350 degrees. Arrange defrosted cauliflower in a lightly greased casserole. Combine milk, water and cornstarch and stir over low heat until well blended and simmering. Pour over the cauliflower, stir in salt and pepper. Sprinkle with cheese and breadcrumbs. Bake uncovered for 15-30 minutes. 4 servings

CAULIFLOWER CASSEROLE

- 1 large head cauliflower, cut into florets
  or equal amounts cauliflower and broccoli
- 1 (10 ¾-ounce) can cream of shrimp soup
- 8 ounces sour cream
- 2 tablespoons butter, melted and divided
- ¼ teaspoon pepper
- ¼ cup dry bread crumbs

Pre-heat oven to 350 degrees. Cook cauliflower in a small amount of boiling water 6-8 minutes or until crisp-tender. Drain well; place florets in a buttered 2-quart casserole dish and set aside. Combine soup, sour cream, 1 tablespoon butter and pepper; stir well. Pour over cauliflower. Combine breadcrumbs with remaining 1 table-spoon butter; stir well. Sprinkle over soup mixture; bake for 20-25 minutes or until bubbly. 6 servings

CHANTILLY RICE

- 3 cups cooked rice
- ½ cup sour cream
- 1 teaspoon salt
- 1-2 dashes ground red pepper
- 1 cup (4-ounces) grated cheddar cheese, divided

Pre-heat oven to 350 degrees. Combine rice, sour cream, salt, pepper and ½ cup cheese. Spoon into a buttered, shallow 1-quart baking dish. Top with remaining cheese. Bake for 20 minutes. 4 servings

CHEESY POTATO CASSEROLE

- 7 medium potatoes (about 2 pounds)
- 1 (8-ounce) can cream of chicken soup
- 2 cups (8-ounces) shredded cheddar cheese
- 3 tablespoons butter, melted
- 1 ½ cups herb-seasoned stuffing mix
- ¼ cup butter, melted
- l small onion, chopped
- ¼ teaspoon pepper
- 1 teaspoon salt

Pre-heat oven to 350 degrees. Cook potatoes in covered boiling water for 30 minutes or until tender. Drain; let cool to touch. Peel and cut into ¼-inch strips, set aside. Combine ¼ cup butter, onion, soup, salt, and pepper in a large bowl; gently stir in potatoes and cheese. Spoon into a lightly greased 13 x 9 x 2-inch baking dish. Combine 3 tablespoons butter and stuffing mix; sprinkle over the potato mixture. Bake, uncovered for 25 minutes or until thoroughly heated. 8 servings

CHEESY VEGETABLE SUPREME

- 1 cup biscuit mix
- ¼ cup milk
- 2 eggs
- ¼ cup finely chopped onion
- 1 package (10-ounces) frozen chopped spinach or broccoli, thawed and drained
- ½ cup grated Parmesan
- 4 ounces Monterey Jack cut into ½-inch cubes
- 1 (12-ounce) carton of cottage cheese
- ½ teaspoon salt
- 2 cloves of garlic, crushed
- 2 eggs

Pre-heat oven to 375 degrees. Grease 12 x 7 x 2-inch baking dish. Mix biscuit mix, milk, 2 eggs and onion and beat with whisk about 20 strokes. Pour into dish. Mix remaining ingredients, blend well and spoon evenly over batter. Bake about 30 minutes until set. Let stand 5 minutes before cutting. 4-6 servings

CORN AND ZUCCHINI SKILLET DISH

- 3 medium ears of corn
- 1 medium onion, quartered and sliced
- 1 red bell pepper, cut into ½-inch squares
- 1 clove garlic, minced
- 2 tablespoons vegetable oil
- 3 medium zucchini, sliced (about 1 pound)
- 1 large tomato, peeled and chopped
- 2 jalapeno peppers, seeded and minced
- 1 ½ teaspoons chopped fresh or ½ teaspoon dried basil
- ½ teaspoon dried Italian seasoning
- ½ teaspoon salt
- ¼ cup grated Parmesan cheese (or more)

Cut corn off the cobs and set aside. Sauté onion, bell pepper, and garlic in oil in a large skillet for 5 minutes. Add zucchini; cook, stirring often for about 7 minutes. Add corn, tomato and next 4 ingredients; cover and cook over low heat, stirring often, about 7 minutes. Sprinkle with Parmesan and serve. Makes 6 side dishes or 3 main-dish servings

CORN CASSEROLE

- 2 (16 ½-ounce) cans yellow cream-style corn
- 2 cups shredded cheddar cheese
- 1 (4-ounce) can chopped green chilies, drained
- ½ cup finely chopped onion
- 1 cup milk
- 2 large eggs, lightly beaten
- 1 cup yellow cornmeal
- 1 ½ teaspoons garlic salt
- ½ teaspoon baking soda
- 1 ½ teaspoons chopped fresh basil, or ½ teaspoon dried

Pre-heat oven to 350 degrees. Combine first 6 ingredients in a large bowl. Combine cornmeal and remaining ingredients; stir into corn mixture. Pour into a lightly greased 11 x 7 x1 ½-inch pan. Add basil. Makes 6 side dishes or 3 main-dish servings baking dish. Bake for 50 minutes or until a knife inserted in the center comes out clean. 8 servings

CORN PUDDING

- 2 cups fresh or canned corn
- 2 eggs, slightly beaten
- 1 teaspoon sugar
- 1 ½ tablespoons butter, melted
- 2 cups scalded milk
- 1 teaspoon salt
- ⅛ teaspoon pepper

Pre-heat oven to 325 degrees. Combine all ingredients. Bake in buttered baking dish until firm. 6 servings

CREAMED CABBAGE

- 1 small head cabbage, shredded
- 1 (12-ounce) can evaporated milk
- 1 cup dry bread crumbs
- 4 tablespoons butter
- 1 tablespoon sugar

Pre-heat oven to 350 degrees. Steam cabbage 10 minutes (till tender-crisp). Place in a greased casserole. Pour milk over cabbage and sprinkle with breadcrumbs and sugar. Dot with butter. Bake for 30 minutes. Remove cover and bake until crumbs brown and the cabbage is tender (about 30 more minutes). 4-6 servings

CREAMED SPINACH

- 1 ½ pounds fresh spinach (about 2 cups cooked and chopped)
- ¼ cup butter
- 3 tablespoons flour
- 1 ¼ cups milk
- ¾ teaspoon salt
- 1 teaspoon sugar
- dash cinnamon or nutmeg

Wash fresh spinach, remove coarse stems, chop into small pieces and place in a large saucepan (You probably don't need to add additional water as there will be enough clinging to the leaves). Cover and cook over medium heat for 5 minutes. Melt butter in a medium saucepan; blend in flour. Stir in milk, salt, sugar and cinnamon or nutmeg. Cook, stirring constantly until sauce thickens and comes to a boil. Add spinach and mix well. 6 servings

EASY CHEESE SOUFFLE

- 5 slices bread, buttered
- ½ pound grated cheddar cheese
- 2 cups milk
- 3 eggs
- 1 teaspoon salt
- 1 teaspoon dry mustard
- ¼ teaspoon dried thyme

DAY AHEAD OR AT LEAST 6 HOURS BEFORE BAKING: Remove crust from bread, and then add with butter and place layers of cheese between slices of bread in 1-quart casserole. Mix milk, eggs, seasonings and pour over bread. Refrigerate over night or at least 6 hours.

Place casserole in pan of water and bake in 350-degree oven for 1 hour. 4 servings

EASY CORN CASSEROLE

- 1 stick butter, melted
- 1 (15-ounce) can cream style corn
- 1 (15-ounce) can whole kernel corn, with juice
- 2 beaten eggs
- 1 (8-ounce) carton sour cream
- 1 box Jiffy corn muffin mix

Pre-heat oven to 350 degrees. Mix all ingredients together. Use corn muffin mix as dry ingredient. Pour into a greased 8-inch casserole dish. Bake for 45–60 minutes. 6-8 servings

EGGPLANT CASSEROLE

- 1 ½ pounds eggplant
- salt
- flour
- ½ cup olive oil
- 2 cups tomato sauce
- 8 ounces thinly sliced Mozzarella cheese
- ½ cup grated Parmesan cheese

Pre-heat oven to 400 degrees. Peel and cut eggplant into ½-inch slices. Sprinkle both sides of eggplant with salt. Spread slices out in one layer for 20-30 minutes, then pat dry. Dip in flour and shake to remove excess. In a heavy skillet heat ¼ cup olive oil until a light haze forms over it. Brown eggplant quickly. Add more oil as needed. Drain browned eggplant on paper towels. Pour ½ cup of tomato sauce into a lightly greased flat baking dish. Layer (in order) eggplant, tomato sauce, Mozzarella and Parmesan cheese, ending with the Parmesan. Cover and bake for 20 minutes. Uncover and bake another 10 minutes. 4-6 servings

EGGPLANT RUSSE

- 4 tablespoons butter
- 2 tablespoons finely chopped onion
- 1 small eggplant, peeled and cubed
- 1 ½ cups sour cream
- 1 ½ cups canned tomatoes
- 1 tablespoon sugar
- 2 tablespoons flour
- salt and pepper to taste

Melt butter in a large skillet. Cook onion and eggplant until lightly brown. Add tomatoes and sugar. Cook until about half the liquid is evaporated. Cover and cook on low heat until eggplant is tender (about 20 minutes). Blend flour and sour cream and add to eggplant mixture. Cook, stirring gently, until just thickened. Season with salt and pepper to taste. 4-6 servings

FRIED GREEN TOMATOES

- 4 large green tomatoes (about 2 pounds)
- ¼ cup sugar
- ¾ cup all purpose flour
- 1 teaspoon salt
- ⅛ teaspoon pepper
- 3 tablespoons bacon drippings
- 6 tablespoons vegetable oil

Remove a thin slice from top and bottom of tomatoes; cut into ¼–inch slices. Layer slices in a small, deep dish, sprinkle each layer with sugar; let stand one hour. Drain tomato slices, reserving sugar mixture. Combine flour, salt and pepper in a shallow dish; dredge tomato slices in mixture. Heat 1 tablespoon bacon drippings and 2 tablespoons oil in a large, cast-iron skillet until hot; add about one-third of tomato slices. Cook 2 to 3 minutes on each side or until golden brown. Drain on paper towels. Repeat process twice until all tomatoes are browned. Drain grease from skillet, reserving 1 tablespoon, and stir in the reserved sugar mixture. Bring to a boil, cook over medium heat, stirring constantly, 1 minute or until slightly thickened. Drizzle over tomato slices and serve immediately. Makes 4 to 6 servings

GARLIC PARSLEY POTATOES

- 3 pounds medium red new potatoes, unpeeled and sliced
- ¼ cup olive oil
- 8 cloves garlic, minced
- 1 teaspoon salt
- ½ teaspoon pepper
- 2 tablespoons chopped fresh parsley, divided

Pre-heat oven to 350 degrees. Combine first 5 ingredients in a large bowl, toss to coat well. Layer ½ of potatoes in a lightly greased 12 x 8 x 2-inch baking dish. Sprinkle ½ parsley over mixture. Layer remaining potatoes. Cover and bake for 45 minutes or until tender. Uncover and sprinkle with remaining parsley. 8 servings

GINGER CARROTS

- 1 pound carrots, thinly sliced
- ¼ cup golden raisins
- ¼ cup butter
- 3 tablespoons honey
- 1 tablespoon lemon juice
- ¼ teaspoon ground ginger
- ¼ cup sliced almonds

Pre-heat oven to 375 degrees. Cook carrots, covered in ½-inch boiling water about 8 minutes or crisp-tender; drain. Place carrots in 1-quart baking dish. Stir in raisins, butter, honey, lemon juice and ginger. Bake, uncovered for 35 minutes; stirring occasionally. Sprinkle with almonds before serving. 4 servings

GOLDEN RICE

- 2 cups cooked rice
- 2 cups (½ pound) shredded cheddar cheese
- 3 cups grated carrot
- 2 eggs, beaten
- ⅔ cup milk
- 1 tablespoon minced onion
- 1 teaspoon salt
- ¼ teaspoon pepper

Pre-heat oven to 350 degrees. Combine all ingredients, stirring well. Spoon into a greased 1 ½ quart casserole. Bake for 1 hour or until set. 6 servings

HARVARD BEETS

- 3 cups diced cooked beets (canned)
- 1 cup beet juice
- 3 tablespoons flour
- 2 tablespoons sugar
- 1 teaspoon salt
- dash of pepper
- ⅓ cup white vinegar

Cook all ingredients, stirring constantly, until smoothly blended and thickened. 6 servings

HERBED SPINACH BAKE

- 1 (10-ounce) package of frozen spinach, cooked and drained
- 2 cups cooked rice
- 1 cup shredded cheddar cheese
- 2 eggs, slightly beaten
- 2 tablespoons butter
- ½ cup milk
- 2 tablespoons chopped onion
- ½ teaspoon Worcestershire sauce
- 1 teaspoon salt
- ¼ teaspoon dried thyme or rosemary

Pre-heat oven to 350 degrees. Cook and drain the frozen spinach and mix with cooked rice. Add remaining ingredients, mixing well. Put into baking dish and bake for 20-25 minutes or until knife inserted in middle comes out clean. May be fixed ahead of time, refrigerated, and then baked at the last minute. 6 servings

HONEY GLAZED CARROTS

- 2 pounds carrots, scraped and thinly sliced
- ½ cup water
- 3 tablespoons honey
- 3 tablespoons brown sugar
- 2 tablespoons butter

Combine carrots and water in a medium saucepan. Bring to a boil; cover, reduce heat, and simmer 8-10 minutes or until crisp-tender. Drain and return to pan. Add honey and remaining ingredients; cook over low heat, stirring gently, until butter and sugar melt. Blend well before serving. 6-8 servings

MARINATED ASPARAGUS

- 2 pounds fresh asparagus
- ¾ cup olive oil
- 1 tablespoon sugar
- ½ cup white balsamic vinegar
- 4 cloves garlic, minced
- 1 teaspoon red pepper flakes

Snap off tough ends of asparagus and cook in boiling water to cover for 3 minutes or until asparagus is crisp-tender; drain. Plunge asparagus into ice water to stop cooking process; drain. Arrange asparagus in a 13 x 9-inch baking dish. Whisk together olive oil, sugar, balsamic vinegar, garlic, and red pepper flakes until well blended; pour over asparagus. Cover and chill 8 hours. Drain before serving. 6-8 servings

MARINATED VEGETABLES

- ½ cup vegetable oil
- ⅓ cup cider vinegar
- 1 ½ teaspoons sugar
- 1 teaspoon dried dill weed
- ½ teaspoon garlic salt
- ¼ teaspoon pepper AND salt
- ½ pound fresh broccoli, stems discarded and head cut into florets
- 1 small cauliflower, stems discarded and head cut into florets
- 3 small yellow squash, thinly sliced
- 3 medium carrots, scraped and diagonally sliced
- 3 medium fresh mushrooms, sliced

Combine first 7 ingredients in a jar. Cover tightly and shake vigorously. Set aside. Combine broccoli, cauliflower, squash, carrots and mushrooms in a large bowl. Pour oil mixture over vegetables, stirring gently; cover and chill 24 hours, stirring occasionally. Recipe easily doubles. 6 servings

MOCK ASPARAGUS SOUFFLE

- 6 thick (¾-inch) slices firm-textured bread (like homemade or bakery French)
- 6 slices of Swiss cheese
- 4 eggs
- 2 cups milk
- 1 teaspoon salt
- ⅛ teaspoon pepper
- ¼ teaspoon ground nutmeg
- 1 tablespoon finely chopped onion
- 18 blanched asparagus spears
- ½ cup shredded cheddar cheese

To blanch asparagus:
Bring to boil a pot of salted water large enough to hold asparagus. Peel stems using a vegetable peeler or sharp knife and trim spears to 6 inches long. Tie asparagus in 2 bundles with kitchen string. Drop in boiling salted water and blanch until tender, but still slightly crunchy. Drain and run under cold water to cool. Dry on paper towels.

Pre-heat oven to 325 degrees. Trim crusts from bread. Arrange slices in bottom of the 13 x 9 x 2-inch pan. Top each bread slice with a slice of Swiss cheese. In a bowl, beat eggs slightly; add milk, stir in seasonings and onion. Pour this mixture over the bread/cheese. Bake for 25 minutes. Remove from oven and top each bread slice with 3 cooked asparagus spears. Sprinkle on shredded cheddar cheese. Return dish to oven and continue to bake for 10-15 minutes, until custard sets and top is golden. Allow to stand 5 minutes before serving. 6 servings

MONASTERY-STYLE LENTILS

- 1 cup dried lentils, washed
- 3 cups water
- ¼ dried thyme
- ¼ teaspoon dried marjoram

Cover and bring to a boil, reduce heat and simmer for 15 minutes. Then add:

- 3 onions, chopped
- 1 carrot, finely chopped
- ¼ cup olive oil

Cook for about 15 minutes more. Then add:

- ¼ cup finely mined fresh parsley
- 1 (14 or 15-ounce) can of stewed tomatoes
- 4 tablespoons dry sherry
- ½ teaspoon salt
- pepper to taste

Simmer for an additional 30-40 minutes. Add the salt and pepper the last few minutes of cooking. 4-6 servings

MRS. HOWARD'S BAKED CABBAGE

- 4 to 5 cups coarsely chopped cabbage
- 1½ teaspoons salt
- ¼ pound grated longhorn cheese
- ¼ pound grated American cheese
- 2 tablespoons butter
- 2 tablespoons flour
- 1½ cups milk
- ½ cup corn flakes, crumbled

Pre-heat oven to 350 degrees. Salt and cook the cabbage with very little water until tender. Drain well. Grease a 3-quart casserole dish. Mix cheeses. Make a medium white sauce by melting butter, adding the flour and stirring for a few minutes, then adding milk and stirring constantly until sauce thickens (about 10 minutes). Alternate a layer of cabbage, a layer of mixed cheeses, then a layer of white sauce. Top with a layer of cheese and sprinkle with corn flake crumbs. Bake uncovered until heated through and cheese is golden brown (about 30 minutes). 6 servings

ONION CASSEROLE

- 2 tablespoons butter
- 2 large sweet onions, peeled, sliced into rings
- ½ pound Swiss cheese, grated
- ¼ teaspoon pepper
- 1 (10 ¾-ounce) can cream of chicken soup
- ¼ cup milk
- buttered fresh bread cut into cubes (for topping)

Pre-heat oven to 350 degrees. Cook onion rings in butter until soft and transparent. Place in a 2-quart casserole and spread evenly with grated cheese. Sprinkle with pepper. Heat soup and milk and pour over onions. Cut through all layers with a knife so soup mixture will seep through. Overlap buttered bread on top. Cook, covered for 45 minutes, uncover and cook another 15 minutes. 8 servings

ONION MUSHROOM CASSEROLE

- 3 medium (8-10 ounces each) sweet onions, sliced
- ½ pound fresh mushrooms, sliced
- 2 tablespoons butter
- 1 cup shredded Swiss cheese
- 4-5 slices French bread (about ½-inch thick)
- 4-5 slices Swiss cheese
- 1 (10 ¾-ounce) can cream of chicken soup
- 5 ounces evaporated milk
- 2 teaspoons soy sauce

Pre-heat oven to 375 degrees. In a large skillet sauté onions and mushrooms in butter until soft; about 5-8 minutes. Place in a lightly greased 9 x 13-inch baking dish. Sprinkle grated Swiss cheese over onions. Arrange bread slices over top and cover each with a slice of Swiss cheese. Combine soup, milk and soy sauce. Pour over mixture to completely cover. Cover and refrigerate overnight. Bake, covered for 30 minutes. Uncover and continue to bake about 10 minutes longer or until heated through. 6-8 servings

ONION PIE

- 1 cup fine saltine cracker crumbs
- (¼ pound)
- ¼ cup melted butter
- 3 cups thinly sliced onions (6 or 7 medium sweet onion)
- 2 tablespoon butter
- ¾ cup milk
- 2 eggs, lightly beaten
- ¾ teaspoon salt
- dash of pepper
- ¼ cup shredded sharp cheddar cheese
- dash of paprika

Pre-heat oven to 350 degrees. Mix cracker crumbs and melted butter and press into the bottom and sides of an 8-inch pie plate. Cook onion in butter; slowly stirring to separate into rings until tender, but not brown. Place in pie shell. Combine milk, eggs, salt and pepper. Pour over onion. Sprinkle pie with shredded cheese, add a dash of paprika. Bake for 30 minutes or until knife inserted into the pie in the middle comes out clean. Serve hot or cold (it reheats well). 6 servings

PICKLED BEETS

- 3 (16-ounce each) cans of sliced beets, juice from all 3 cans
- 2 cups cider vinegar
- 1 ¼ cup sugar
- 2 teaspoons salt
- 4-5 teaspoons pickling spices
- 6 whole cloves
- 3 medium onions, sliced

Combine the liquids, sugar, and salt with spices which have been placed in a loose tea holder. Heat to boiling. Add beets and onions and simmer 5-10 minutes. Place in a large (48-ounce) pickle jar and refrigerate.

POLENTA

- 3 cups water
- ½ teaspoon salt
- 1 cup cornmeal *
- 2 tablespoons butter
- ⅛ teaspoon crushed red pepper flakes (optional)
- ½ cup grated Parmesan cheese

In a saucepan, bring the water and salt to a boil. Add the cornmeal in a thin, steady stream while whisking briskly. Stir in butter and optional crushed red pepper flakes. Simmer for about 10 minutes, stirring often, until thickened. Polenta sputters as it cooks, so cover the pan when you're not stirring. Remove from heat, stir in Parmesan and serve. 3 cups

*Finely ground cornmeal cooks very rapidly, about 5 minutes. Coarse-textured cornmeal will take longer to cook but many people prefer its texture.

BAKED POLENTA WITH GORGONZOLA

- 1 ⅔ cups cornmeal
- 6 ¼ cups salted water
- 6 tablespoons butter
- pepper
- ½ pound Gorgonzola

Pre-heat oven to 425 degrees. Make Polenta as described in the Polenta recipe on page 133 with the cornmeal and 6 ¼ cups salted water. When it is done, stir in the butter and pepper. Pour a layer of hot Polenta into a buttered ovenproof dish, cover with a layer of cheese, then add another layer of Polenta, another of cheese, and finish with the Polenta. Bake until browned. May vary by using Taleggio or Fontina instead of Gorgonzola. For a "pasticcio di polenta" add alternating layers of a thick tomato sauce. 4 servings

POTATO SOUFFLE

- 1 cup milk
- ¼ cup butter
- 3 cups mashed potatoes *
- ½ cup grated cheddar cheese
- 1 teaspoon salt
- 1 teaspoon dry mustard
- 2 egg yolks
- 2 egg whites

Pre-heat oven to 350 degrees. Beat milk and butter together in a large pot. Stir in mashed potatoes, beat until light and fluffy. Beat in cheddar cheese, salt and dry mustard. Separate eggs. Beat yolks until thick and fold into the potato mixture. Beat egg whites until stiff and fold into potato mixture. Turn mixture into a greased 1 ½ quart baking dish. Bake about 45-50 minutes. Serve immediately. 6-8 servings

*Good way to use leftover mashed potatoes.

ROASTED SUCCOTASH

- 1 ½ cups fresh corn kernels (about three ears)
- 1 cup chopped red bell pepper
- ½ cup chopped onion
- 1 teaspoon ground cumin
- 1 cup chopped yellow squash
- 1 ½ tablespoon olive oil
- 2 garlic cloves, minced
- ½ cup low-sodium chicken broth
- 2 tablespoons chopped fresh cilantro
- ½ teaspoon salt
- ⅛ teaspoon pepper
- ⅛ teaspoon hot sauce
- 1 (10-ounce) package frozen baby lima beans, thawed

Cook first four ingredients in a nonstick skillet over high heat, stirring occasionally, five minutes or until slightly blackened. Add squash, oil, and garlic; saute over medium-high heat one minute. Add broth and remaining ingredients; cook two minutes or until thoroughly heated, stirring often. 5-6 servings

SMOTHERED CABBAGE WEDGES

- 1 medium cabbage
- ½ cup finely chopped green pepper
- ¼ cup finely chopped onion
- ¼ cup butter, melted
- ¼ cup all-purpose flour
- 2 cups milk
- ½ teaspoon salt
- ⅛ teaspoon pepper
- ½ cup mayonnaise or salad dressing
- ¾ cup (3-ounces) shredded medium cheddar cheese
- 3 tablespoons chili sauce

Pre-heat oven to 375 degrees. Cut cabbage into 8 wedges, remove core; cover and cook 10 minutes in a small amount of lightly salted boiling water. Drain well and place cabbage in a 13 x 9 x 2-inch baking dish. Sauté green pepper and onion in butter until tender but not brown. Add flour and cook one minute, stirring constantly. Gradually add milk, cook over medium heat, stirring constantly, until thickened and bubbly. Stir in salt and pepper. Pour sauce over cabbage. Bake for 20 minutes. Combine mayonnaise, cheese and chili sauce, mix well. Spoon sauce over cabbage wedges and bake an additional 5 minutes. 8 servings

SOUTHWESTERN BAKED BEANS

- 2 (15-ounces each) cans dark red kidney beans
- 1 (16-ounces) can black beans
- 1 (19-ounces) can white kidney beans
- 1 (28-ounces) can Italian plum tomatoes, drained and chopped
- 1 cup yellow onion, chopped
- 2 large cloves of garlic, chopped
- ¼ cup dark molasses
- ¼ cup cider vinegar
- 2 tablespoons honey
- 2 teaspoons dried oregano
- 2 teaspoons dry mustard
- 2 teaspoons ground cumin
- 1 ½ teaspoons ground ginger
- 1 teaspoon chili powder
- pinch of crushed red-pepper flakes
- salt, to taste

Pre-heat oven to 350 degrees. Rinse and drain beans, mix, and place in a large casserole dish. Add remaining ingredients to the casserole, folding together gently so that the beans don't break up. Bake, covered, for 45 minutes. Remove cover; stir and bake, uncovered 30 minutes more or until hot and bubbly. 8-10 servings

SPINACH AND RICE CASSEROLE

- ½ stick unsalted butter
- 3 cups cooked rice
- 4 large eggs, beaten lightly
- 1 cup milk
- ¾ pound (about 3 cups) sharp cheddar, grated
- 1 (10-ounce) package frozen chopped spinach, cooked and drained
- 1 tablespoon finely chopped onion
- 1 tablespoon Worcestershire sauce
- ½ teaspoon salt, or to taste
- ¼ teaspoon dried thyme, crumbled
- ¼ teaspoon rosemary, crumbled
- ¼ teaspoon marjoram, crumbled

Pre-heat oven to 350 degrees. In a large saucepan melt butter over low heat and stir in remaining ingredients. Spread mixture in a lightly greased 2-quart casserole and set casserole in a larger pan. Fill pan with enough hot water to reach halfway up sides of casserole. Bake casserole in middle of oven for 45-55 minutes, or until set. 8 servings

SPINACH BAKE

- 1 (14 or 15-ounce) can spinach
- 4 eggs, beaten
- 1 cup milk
- 1 cup shredded Swiss cheese
- 1 cup cubed firm white bread
- ½ cup sliced green onions
- ¼ cup grated Parmesan cheese

Pre-heat oven to 375 degrees. Drain canned spinach squeezing out excess liquid. Combine all ingredients; pour into a 1-quart baking dish. Cover and bake for 25-30 minutes or until tests done with knife. 6 servings

SPINACH NOODLES

- 1 (14-ounce) can spinach
- 1 (8-ounce) package medium egg noodles
- 2 tablespoons chopped onion
- 1 clove garlic, crushed
- 1 tablespoon butter, melted
- ¼ cup butter
- ½ cup whipping cream
- 1 cup grated Parmesan cheese
- coarsely ground black pepper

Drain spinach in a colander; place on paper towels and press until spinach is barely moist. Cook noodles according to package directions; drain well. Sauté onion and garlic in 1 tablespoon butter until tender; stir in spinach. Cover and simmer 3 minutes. Add ¼ cup butter to warm noodles, tossing gently until butter melts. Add spinach mixture, whipping cream, and cheese; toss gently. Sprinkle with pepper. 8 servings

STEWED TOMATOES

- 1 large (28-ounce) can stewed tomatoes
- 4 tablespoons flour
- ½ cup milk
- 3-4 tablespoons sugar (more if desired)
- salt and pepper to taste

Place tomatoes in medium saucepan. Blend flour with milk until smooth and add to tomatoes along with sugar (to taste). Simmer until well blended, stirring occasionally. May add croutons or cubes of stale bread, if desired. 4-6 servings

SWEET POTATOES WITH PECANS

- 4 large sweet potatoes or yams
- ½ stick butter, softened
- ¾ cup sugar
- ⅛ teaspoon salt
- ¼ cup good bourbon whiskey
- ½ cup pecans, coarsely chopped

Pre-heat oven to 325 degrees. Place sweet potatoes in a large saucepan and add enough water to cover completely. Bring the water to a boil, cover, and cook until the potatoes are tender, about 35 minutes. Drain. When the potatoes are cool enough to handle, peel off the skins. Place the potatoes in a mixing bowl and mash with the butter. Beat in the sugar, salt and whiskey. Spread half the potato mixture in a greased 1 ½ quart casserole and sprinkle with half the pecans. Repeat the layers. Bake for about 30 minutes or until heated thoroughly. 6-8 servings

SWISS BROCCOLI CASSEROLE

- 2 packages (10-ounces each) frozen broccoli spears, cooked and drained
- 3 hard boiled eggs, sliced
- 1 (10 ¾-ounce) can cream of celery soup
- ⅔ cup milk
- 3-ounces of canned French fried onions
- ½ cup (2-ounces) shredded Swiss cheese

Pre-heat oven to 350 degrees. Combine soup and milk. Arrange broccoli in an 8 x 12-inch baking dish. Layer eggs, ½ of French fried onions, soup mixture and cheese over broccoli. Bake for 25 minutes. Top with remaining onions and bake 5 minutes longer. 6 servings

TOMATO AND ZUCCHINI TART

- 1 packaged refrigerated piecrust
- 1 medium zucchini, thinly sliced (about ¾ pound)
- 2 teaspoon olive oil
- 3 medium plum tomatoes, sliced
- ½ cup fresh basil, chopped
- ⅓ cup grated Parmesan cheese
- ⅓ cup mayonnaise
- ½ teaspoon pepper

Pre-heat oven to 450 degrees. Fit piecrust into a 9-inch tart pan. Prick bottom and sides of piecrust with a fork. Bake piecrust at 450 degrees until lightly brown (about 9-11 minutes). Let cool. Sauté zucchini in hot oil in a large skillet about 2 minutes or until tender. Arrange zucchini in bottom of prepared crust. Arrange tomatoes on top of zucchini. Stir together basil, cheese, and mayonnaise. Spread gently and evenly over top of tomatoes. Sprinkle with pepper. Bake for 10-15 minutes or until heated and cheese is slightly melted. 8 servings

TOMATOES WITH PESTO

- 6 medium plum tomatoes
- 3 tablespoons pesto
  (see recipes for 2 pesto recipes on page 166)

Pre-heat oven to 450 degrees. Cut tomatoes in half lengthwise. Cut a thin slice off the bottom of each half so they will sit flat. Place tomato halves in 2-quart baking dish. Spread pesto on tomatoes almost to edges. Bake 12-15 minutes until tomatoes are hot and slightly softened. 6-8 servings

TOMATO-SQUASH CASSEROLE

- 4 medium summer squash (or cucumbers) unpeeled
- 2-3 ripe tomatoes, peeled and chopped
- 6 slices of bacon, fried and crumbled or 1 ½ cup real bacon bits
- 1 ½ cups (8 slices) American cheese, shredded
- 1 small onion, chopped
- ½ teaspoon salt
- ½ cup fine breadcrumbs
- 2 tablespoons butter

Pre-heat oven to 375 degrees. Parboil squash until skin tender (about 5-10 minutes). After removing squash dip tomatoes in the hot water to loosen skin and peel. Slice parboiled squash thinly and combine rest of ingredients except breadcrumbs and butter. Place in a lightly greased baking dish. Top with breadcrumbs and dot with butter. Bake for about 35 minutes or until cheese has melted and thoroughly heated. 6-8 servings

ZUCCHINI GRATIN

- 2 tablespoons olive oil
- 2 cloves garlic, peeled
- 2 sprigs fresh thyme
- 6 medium zucchini, about 1½ pounds, peeled and thinly sliced into rounds
- 3 cups cooked long-grain rice, room temperature
- 3 large eggs
- 1 cup heavy cream
- ¼ cup grated Swiss cheese

Pre-heat oven to 350 degrees. Heat olive oil in skillet over medium heat. Add garlic, 1 sprig thyme and zucchini. Sauté, stirring frequently until zucchini is tender (about 8 minutes). Remove pan from heat. Discard garlic and thyme sprig. Set aside. Place rice in a bowl. Mix in eggs, cream, remaining thyme leaves*, and zucchini. Spread mixture evenly in a 10-inch gratin dish. Sprinkle Swiss cheese on top. Bake until top is brown and crisp (about 20-25 minutes). Remove from oven. Set aside for 15 minutes. Serve warm or at room temperature. 6-8 servings

* If fresh thyme is not available add approximately 1 teaspoon dried thyme (or to taste) at this point.

ZUCCHINI PIE

- 2 cups shredded zucchini
- ¾ cup biscuit mix
- ¾ cup (3-ounces) shredded cheddar cheese
- 1 small onion, chopped
- ½ teaspoon salt
- ¼ teaspoon pepper
- ¼ teaspoon dried sage
- 2 large eggs, lightly beaten
- ¼ cup vegetable oil

Pre-heat oven to 350 degrees. Stir together all ingredients. Pour into a greased 9-inch pie plate. Bake for 45 minutes. Cool 10 minutes before serving. 4-6 servings

APPETIZERS

BAKED GOUDA CHEESE

- 1 (7-ounce) round natural Gouda cheese
- 1 (8-ounce) can refrigerator crescent dinner rolls
- 1 egg, beaten

Preheat oven to 350 degrees. Cut cheese round in half crosswise to form 2 circles, remove wax. Separate dough into 4 rectangles; firmly press perforations to seal. Place 1 rectangle on top of a 2nd, repeat with remaining rectangles making 2 double-thick rectangles. Press each into a 6-inch square; place cheese circle in the center of each. Pull corners of dough to top of cheese. Press dough tightly against cheese. Twist dough in center to seal, twisting off excess dough. Press seams to seal. Repeat with 2nd Gouda wrap. If desired, cut out decorative shapes from excess dough and place on top of each Gouda wrap. Brush with beaten egg. Place 3-inches apart on an ungreased cookie sheet. Bake for 18-22 minutes or until golden brown. Cool 10 minutes before serving. 8 servings

CHEESE BALL

- 16 ounces cream cheese, softened
- 2 tablespoons chopped green pepper
- 2 tablespoons chopped onion
- ¼ cup drained crushed pineapple
- 2 teaspoons seasoning salt
- 1 cup chopped pecans

Mix all ingredients together well and form a ball. Roll cheese ball in 1 cup chopped pecans. Chill at least 2 hours before serving. 1 cheese ball

CHEESE WAFERS
COPPER PENNIES

- ½ cup butter
- ½ pound shredded sharp cheddar cheese
- 1 cup flour
- ½ package dry onion soup mix
- ½ teaspoon salt

Pre-heat oven to 375 degrees. Allow butter and cheese to come to room temperature and mix thoroughly. Add remaining ingredients and blend. Shape into 3 rolls about 1-inch in diameter. Wrap in foil and chill. Cut into ¼-inch slices. Place on a greased cookie sheet and bake for 10-12 minutes (check carefully as it burns easily) Store in air tight container. About 100 "pennies"

FRUIT PIZZA

- 1 package Pillsbury sugar cookie dough
- 11 ounces cream cheese, room temperature
- 2 tablespoon sugar
- 2-3 bananas, sliced
- 1 can cherry pie filling
- 1 small can crushed pineapple, juice drained, but saved

Pre-heat oven to 375 degrees. Let cookie dough set at room temperature until easy to manage. Spread on a lightly greased large pizza pan. Bake for 10-12 minutes. Let cool completely. To softened cream cheese add the sugar and enough pineapple juice to spread easily. Cover baked crust with mixture. Place about 2-inches cherry pie filling on outside rim of crust. In the middle place the bananas (about 3 deep). Place the crushed pineapple in the center, Chill until ready to serve. You may vary the fruit and pie filling, i.e. blueberry pie filling, sliced strawberries and pineapple for July 4th, etc. 8-10 servings

GARLIC SNACK CRACKERS

- 24 ounces of oyster crackers
- 2 (1-ounce) packages of Hidden Valley Ranch Dressing Mix
- 1 cup cooking oil
- ½ teaspoon garlic powder
- 1 teaspoon dill weed

Mix all ingredients and pour over crackers. Stir every half hour for 2 hours. Store in airtight container. Good snack or serve with soup/chili.

GOLDEN NUT CRUNCH

- 12 ounces dry roasted mixed nuts or peanuts
- ¼ cup UNSALTED butter, melted
- ¼ cup Parmesan cheese
- ¼ teaspoon garlic powder
- ¼ teaspoon oregano
- ¼ teaspoon celery salt
- 4 cups Golden Grahams cereal

Preheat oven to 300 degrees. Mix nuts and butter in a bowl until nuts well coated. Add cheese, garlic powder, oregano, and celery salt. Toss until well coated. Spread on an un-greased jelly roll pan. Bake, stirring occasionally about 15 minutes. Stir in cereal. Cool. Store in an airtight container. About 6 ½ cups

PARMESAN-SPINACH SPREAD

- 1 (10-ounce) package frozen chopped spinach, thawed
- 1 ¼ cups grated Parmesan cheese, divided
- ¼ cup finely chopped onion
- 3 ounces cream cheese, soft
- ¾ cup mayonnaise
- 1 teaspoon Tabasco sauce
- 1 teaspoon dried Italian herbs
- ½ teaspoon garlic powder
- ¼ teaspoon pepper
- 1 teaspoon paprika

Pre-heat oven to 350 degrees. Squeeze excess moisture from thawed spinach. Combine spinach, 1 cup Parmesan cheese and next 7 ingredients. Spoon into a greased 1-quart baking dish. Bake for 10 minutes. Sprinkle with remaining ¼ cup Parmesan cheese and paprika; bake an additional 10 minutes. Serve with crackers or party rye. About 2 ½ cups

ROQUEFORT CHEESE

- 1 cup cottage cheese
- ½ cup mayonnaise
- ¼ cup crumbled Roquefort cheese

Place all ingredients in a bowl and whip with electric mixer until smooth. This is an excellent dressing for head lettuce salad or may be used as a dip for chips or crackers.

RUMAKI

- ¼ pound chicken livers, trimmed and rinsed
- ¼ cup soy sauce
- 1 tablespoon finely grated peeled fresh ginger
- 2 tablespoons packed light brown sugar
- ½ teaspoon curry powder
- 12 canned water chestnut, drained and halved horizontally
- 8 bacon slices (½) pound cut crosswise into thirds
- 24 wooden toothpicks

Cut chicken livers into 24 (about ½-inch) pieces. Mix together soy sauce, ginger, brown sugar, and curry powder. Add livers and water chestnuts and toss to coat. Marinate, covered and chilled for 1 hour. While livers marinate, soak toothpicks in cold water 1 hour. Drain well. Remove livers and chestnuts from marinade and discard marinade. Wrap 1 piece of liver and 1 water chestnut with 1 piece of bacon and secure with a toothpick. Broil rumaki on rack of a broiler pan 2-inches from heat, turning once, until bacon is crisp and livers are cooked but still slightly pink inside, about 5-6 minutes. Serve immediately. 24 hors d'oeuvres

Another simple hors d'oeuvre: Wrap 1 date and 1 water chestnut with bacon and broil until bacon is crisp. May serve hot or cold.

SAUSAGE SNACK WRAPS

- 2 (8-ounce) cans refrigerated crescent dinner rolls
- 48 fully cooked cocktail smoked sausage links or hot dogs

Preheat oven to 375 degrees. Separate dough into 8 triangles. Cut each triangle lengthwise into thirds. Place sausages on shortest side of each triangle. Roll up, starting at the shortest side and rolling to the opposite point. Place on un-greased cookie sheets. Bake for 12-15 minutes or until golden brown. Serve warm with catsup and mustard, if desired. 48 snacks

SHRIMP MOLD

- 1 envelope Knox gelatin
- 2 cans baby shrimp (drained but reserve ¼ cup juice)
- 1 (10 ¾-ounce) can cream of shrimp soup
- 8 ounces cream cheese
- 1 cup mayonnaise
- ½ cup minced green onion
- ½ cup celery
- ½ cup green pepper

Heat juice and gelatin. Melt cream cheese into mixture. Add rest of ingredients. Grease a salad mold with cooking spray. Add mixture, cover, and refrigerate until firm. May serve slice on lettuce as an appetizer or use on crackers as a spread.

SOUTHWEST DEVILED EGGS

- 1 dozen hard-cooked eggs*
- ½ cup instant potato flakes
- ⅓ cup mayonnaise
- ⅓ cup milk
- 1 tablespoon prepared mustard
- ½ teaspoon salt
- 1 (4 ½-ounce) can diced green chilies
- ¾ cup real (or imitation) bacon bits
- ¾ cup (3-ounces) shredded cheddar, Monterey Jack, or taco cheese blend

Cut eggs in half lengthwise, remove yolks; set whites aside. Beat egg yolks, potato flakes, mayonnaise, milk, mustard and salt at medium speed with an electric mixer 1-2 minutes or until fluffy. Stir in green chilies, bacon bits and cheese. Spoon mixture into egg whites; cover and chill. Makes 2 dozen.

*I put eggs in water over medium heat. Bring to a boil. Cover and remove from heat. Let stand for 11 minutes, then cool in cold water immediately.

VEGETABLE PIZZA

- 2 packages refrigerated crescent rolls
- 1 (8-ounce) package cream cheese, softened
- ½ cup mayonnaise
- 1 package original Ranch dressing mix
- 6 cups mixed vegetables, chopped

Pre-heat oven to 375 degrees. Flatten crescent rolls in a pizza pan or 10 x 15-inch cookie sheet. Bake for 7 to 9 minutes. Cool completely. Mix cream cheese and Ranch dressing mix and spread over crescent rolls. Add 6 cups of mixed chopped vegetables (celery, green onion, green pepper, broccoli, cauliflower, carrots, mushrooms, tomatoes, etc.) Chill and serve.

BREADS

BETTY O'SHEA'S IRISH SODA BREAD

- 4 cups sifted flour
- 3 teaspoons baking powder
- 1 teaspoon salt
- ¾ teaspoon baking soda
- ¼ cup sugar
- 1 cup buttermilk (more, if needed)
- 2 tablespoons caraway seeds
- 2 cups raisins (or more)
- ¼ pound butter (one stick)
- 1 egg
- 1 egg beaten

Preheat oven to 350 degrees. Sift flour, baking powder, salt, sugar, and baking soda. Stir in caraway seeds. Cut in butter and mix well with fingers until consistency of oatmeal. Stir in raisins. Combine buttermilk and egg. Add to flour mixture and mix with wooden spoon. Turn dough onto a floured board. Knead lightly and shape into a ball. Place in a greased, floured baking dish. Cut a deep cross onto the top. Brush top with slightly beaten egg. Bake one hour. Cool for 5 minutes before removing from baking dish. Cool well before slicing. 1 loaf

BRAN MUFFINS

- 15 ounces Raisin Bran cereal
- 5 cups all purpose flour
- 2-3 cups sugar
- 5 teaspoons baking soda
- 2 teaspoon salt
- 4 eggs, beaten
- 1 quart buttermilk
- 1 cup vegetable oil

Pre-heat oven to 400 degrees. Combine dry ingredients in large mixing bowl. Add liquid ingredients and stir until well moistened. Store in a covered container in the refrigerator at least 3 days before using. Batter lasts 6 weeks refrigerated. Grease muffin tins and fill ⅔ full. Bake for 12-15 minutes. Use batter as desired. Makes about 4 dozen muffins.

CARAWAY/RAISIN
SODA BREAD ROLLS

- 3 ½ cups cake flour
- ½ cup sugar
- 1 ½ teaspoons baking soda
- ¾ teaspoon salt
- ½ cup (1 stick) chilled unsalted butter, cut into ½-inch pieces
- ½ cup golden raisins
- 1 tablespoon caraway seeds
- 1 cup milk (do not use nonfat or low-fat)

Pre-heat oven to 400 degrees. Lightly butter baking sheet. Mix flour, sugar, baking soda and salt in a large bowl. Add butter and rub in with fingertips until mixture resembles course meal. Mix in raisins and caraway seeds. Using fork, mix in milk, stirring until moist clumps form. Using floured hands and ⅓ cup dough for each, shape dough into 12 balls. Transfer to prepared baking sheet. Flatten into 2 ½-inch diameter, 1-inch rounds. Cut shallow cross in top of rounds. Bake rolls until golden brown and toothpick inserted in center comes out clean, about 20 minutes. Serve rolls warm or at room temperature. 12 rolls

CHEDDAR APPLE BREAD

- 2 ½ cups flour
- ¾ cup sugar
- 2 teaspoons baking powder
- ½ teaspoon salt
- ½ teaspoon cinnamon (or a little more, if you like cinnamon as I do)
- 2 eggs, beaten
- ¾ cup milk
- ⅓ cup butter, melted
- 2 cups shredded sharp cheddar cheese
- 1½ cups peeled and chopped apples
- ¾ cup chopped nuts

Pre-heat oven to 350 degrees. Combine dry ingredients. Add combined eggs, milk and butter, mix well. Stir in remaining ingredients. Spoon into well-greased and floured 9 x 5-inch loaf pan. Bake for 65 to 70 minutes or until tooth pick inserted in center comes out clean. Let stand 5 minutes before removing from pan. 1 loaf

CHEESE BISCUITS

- 1 pound sharp cheddar cheese
- 1 pound butter
- 4 cups un-sifted flour
- pinch of salt
- 1 egg, beaten
- Pecan or walnut halves

Preheat oven to 375 degrees. Grate cheese, mix with flour and salt, then work in butter. Roll to desired thickness (about ⅛-inch). Cut with a small, round cookie cutter. Place a nut half on each biscuit and brush with beaten egg to make a glaze. Bake about 10 minutes. 24 biscuits

CHEESY ZUCCHINI AND ONION FLATBREAD

- non-stick vegetable oil spray
- 1 (10-ounce) tube refrigerator pizza dough
- ¾ cup garlic and herb cheese spread, divided
- ¾ cup finely grated Parmesan cheese, divided
- 3 tablespoons chopped fresh Italian parsley, divided
- 1 small red onion
- 1 (7 or 8-inch) long zucchini, cut crosswise into ⅛-inch thick rounds, divided
- olive oil
- salt and pepper, to taste

Preheat oven to 400 degrees. Line a baking sheet with parchment paper; spray with cooking spray. Unroll dough onto parchment. Spread half of the herb cheese over 1 long half of dough, leaving ½-inch plain border. Sprinkle with half of Parmesan and 2 tablespoons parsley. Using parchment as an aid, fold plain half of dough over filled half, but do not seal the edges. Spread remaining herb cheese over top; sprinkle with remaining Parmesan. Slice onion in ⅛ thin rounds. Arrange 1 row of zucchini down 1 long side of dough. Arrange onion rounds in row alongside zucchini. Arrange 1 more row of zucchini along side onion. Brush vegetables with oil; sprinkle with salt and pepper. Bake until puffed and brown at edges, about 24 minutes. Sprinkle with 1 tablespoon chopped parsley before serving. 4-6 servings

CRANBERRY PUMPKIN BREAD

- 3 ½ cups all-purpose flour
- 1 ½ cups sugar
- 2 teaspoons pumpkin pie spice
- 1 teaspoon baking soda
- 1 teaspoon baking powder
- ¾ teaspoon salt
- 1 (16-ounce) can whole berry cranberry sauce
- 1 (15-ounce) can solid-packed pumpkin
- ¾ cup chopped pecans
- ⅔ cup vegetable oil
- 4 eggs

Glaze:
- 1 cup confectioner's sugar
- ¼ cup orange juice concentrate
- ⅛ teaspoon ground allspice

Pre-heat oven to 350 degrees. In a large bowl, combine flour, sugar, pie spice, baking soda, baking powder and salt. In another bowl, combine the cranberry sauce, pumpkin, pecans, oil and eggs; stir into dry ingredients and mix well. Pour into two greased 9 x 5 x 3-inch loaf pans. Bake for 65 minutes or until toothpick inserted in thecenter comes out clean. Cool for 10 minutes; remove from pans to a wire rack to cool completely. Combine glaze ingredients; drizzle over loaves. Makes two loaves.

EASY CHEESE BISCUITS

- ¼ cup butter, softened
- 2 cups self-rising flour
- 1 cup buttermilk
- 1 ½ cups (6-ounces) shredded cheddar cheese

Pre-heat oven to 425 degrees. Cut butter into the flour until mixture resembles coarse crumbs, add remaining ingredients and stir well. Drop by the tablespoon, 2 inches apart onto a large, greased baking sheet. Bake for 12-15 minutes or until golden. About 1 ½ dozen

OATMEAL BANANA BREAD

- 1 ¼ cups oats
- 2 cups biscuit mix
- 3 eggs
- ½ cup brown sugar
- ⅓ cup vegetable oil
- 1 teaspoon vanilla
- 1 ½ cups (3 medium) mashed ripe bananas
- 3 tablespoons plain yogurt
- ¼ cup chopped pecans (optional)

Pre-heat oven to 350 degrees. Stir together oats and biscuit mix. In mixing bowl beat eggs. Add sugar, oil and vanilla. Combine yogurt and bananas, add to egg mixture alternately with dry ingredients. Stir in nuts. Spoon batter into a greased 9 x 5 x 3-inch loaf pan. Bake for 55-50 minutes or until knife inserted through center comes out clean. Cool in pan for 10 minutes, then on rack until thoroughly cool. Wrap loaf and store overnight in refrigerator for flavor to develop. Good served with cream cheese mixed with honey as spread. 1 loaf

ORANGE BREAD

- 2 cups all purpose flour
- 1 teaspoon baking soda
- 1 teaspoon baking powder
- 2 tablespoons butter
- ½ teaspoon salt
- 2 tablespoons orange rind, grated
- 2 teaspoon vanilla
- 1 egg, beaten
- ½ cup orange juice
- 1 cup sugar
- ½ cup boiling water

Pre-heat oven to 350 degrees. Mix dry ingredients. Melt butter in boiling water and blend in orange rind, salt, vanilla, egg, orange juice, and sugar. Then add to dry ingredients and mix well. Pour into a large greased loaf pan and bake for about 1 hour or until knife inserted in middle comes out clean. Slice thin and serve with cream cheese softened with orange juice. 1 large loaf

PEAR ZUCCHINI BREAD

- nonstick cooking spray
- 2 cups all-purpose flour
- 1 cup rye flour
- 2 teaspoons pumpkin pie spice
- 1 teaspoon baking soda
- ½ teaspoon baking powder
- ½ teaspoon salt
- 2 cups chopped, peeled pears or 29-ounce can pear halves, drained and chopped
- 1 cup sugar
- 1 cup packed brown sugar
- 1 cup finely shredded, unpeeled zucchini
- 1 cup cooking oil
- 3 eggs
- 1 tablespoon vanilla
- ½ cup chopped pecans

Pre-heat oven to 350 degrees. Spray two 8 x 4 x 2-inch baking pans with nonstick coating; set aside. In a medium mixing bowl combine flours, pumpkin pie spice, baking soda, baking power and salt. In a large mixing bowl, combine pears, sugars, zucchini, oil, eggs and vanilla: mix well. Add flour mixture; stir just until combined. Stir in chopped nuts. Pour batter into prepared pans. Bake for 50 to 60 minutes or until a toothpick inserted near the center comes out clean. Cool for 10 minutes on a wire rack. Remove bread from pan; cool thoroughly on rack. Wrap in plastic wrap and store overnight before slicing. Makes 2 loaves.

QUICK LITTLE CHEESE BREADS

- 2 eggs, beaten
- ¾ cup water
- 11 ounces of baking mix (Bisquick)
- 2 teaspoons dry mustard
- 1 cup (plus) shredded sharp cheddar cheese
- butter

Preheat oven to 400 degrees. Grease and flour 4 small (about 4 x 2 x 2-inch) loaf pans. Mix eggs, water, Bisquick until un-lumpy. Add dry mustard and cheddar and mix well. Pour into loaf pans and sprinkle tops with a little more cheese, dot with butter. Bake about 25 minutes or until tops are golden brown. 4 small loaves (nice gift size)

SWEET POTATO MUFFINS

- 1 ¾ cups all-purpose flour
- 1 teaspoon baking soda
- ½ teaspoon ground cinnamon
- ¼ teaspoon salt
- 2 eggs
- 1 cup sugar
- ½ cup firmly packed brown sugar
- ½ cup vegetable oil
- 1 (17-ounce) can sweet potatoes, drained and mashed
- ½ cup chopped pecans
- 1 cup dates, chopped
- ¼ cup all-purpose flour

Pre-heat oven to 350 degrees. Combine first 4 ingredients in a large bowl; make a well in center of mixture. Combine eggs and next 4 ingredients in a bowl; beat at medium speed with an electric mixer until blended. Add sweet potato mixture to dry ingredients; stir until moist. Dredge pecans and dates in ¼ cup flour; fold into muffin mixture. Spoon into greased muffin tins, filling ¾ full. Bake for 27-30 minute. Remove from pans immediately. (May bake in miniature muffin tins for 12-14 minutes and makes about 4 dozen). 1 ½ dozen

WHOLE WHEAT BREAD (BILLIE MAE'S)

- 1 ½ cups water
- 1 cup cottage cheese
- ½ cup honey
- ¼ cup butter
- 2 tablespoons sugar
- 3 teaspoons salt
- 2 packages dry yeast
- 1 egg
- 2 cups regular flour
- 2 cups whole-wheat flour
- 4 cups all-purpose flour

Pre-heat oven to 375 degrees. Heat in a large pan until very warm the first four ingredients. Mix the sugar, salt, dry yeast and egg. Add 2 cups regular flour and mix well. Add water, cottage cheese, honey and butter and mix well. Add the 2 cups whole-wheat flour and 4 cups all-purpose flour and beat 2 minutes at medium speed with mixer. Add more all-purpose flour until the dough is not sticky. Knead about 2 minutes, form into 2 loaves in pans. Bake about 35-40 minutes. 2 loaves

ZUCCHINI BREAD

- 3 eggs beaten until foamy
- 1 cup vegetable oil
- 2 cups sugar
- 2 cups grated peeled zucchini
- 1 tablespoon vanilla
- 1 teaspoon baking soda
- ¼ teaspoon (generous) baking powder
- 1 tablespoon cinnamon
- 1 teaspoon salt (optional)
- ½ to 1 cup chopped walnuts or pecans (optional)
- ½ to 1 cup raisins (optional)
- 3 cups all purpose flour

Pre-heat oven to 350 degrees Mix together eggs and dry ingredients; add remaining ingredients, mixing well but DO NOT beat. Divide batter between 2 large greased loaf pans. Bake for approximately 1 hour or until knife inserted in middle comes out clean. Freezes well. 2 loaves

SAUCES & DRESSINGS

BARBECUE SAUCE

- 1 cup beer
- 1 ½ cups chili sauce
- 2 tablespoons grated onion
- 2 tablespoons white vinegar
- 2 teaspoons sugar
- 2 tablespoons Worcestershire sauce
- 2 teaspoons chili powder

Combine all ingredients in a saucepan; bring to a boil and cook about 2 minutes. Delicious as a basting sauce for chicken, spareribs or wieners. About 3 cups

END-OF-THE-HERB-GARDEN TOMATO SAUCE

- 10 pounds very ripe tomatoes
- 1 pound Bermuda onions
- ½ pound sweet green or red peppers
- 2 cups roughly chopped celery with leaves
- about 1 quart mixed herb sprigs or leaves (see below)
- ¼ cup vinegar
- ½ cup sugar
- salt and pepper to taste
- Herbs to use if you have them: oregano, majoram, thyme, basil, sage, parsley and chive.

Quarter tomatoes and put them into a large, non-aluminum pot. Roughly chop onions and peppers and add to pot. Add 2 cups water, place celery and herbs on top, cover and simmer for about 3 hours, stirring occasionally. Put vegetables in blender in small batches and puree. Return puree to heat, add vinegar, sugar, and simmer uncovered for about an hour. Stir frequently. Sauce should become fairly thick. Reduce it further if you want a thicker sauce. Season to taste. Cool and freeze.

Note: Makes about 2 quarts (which I freeze in ice-cube trays, then put into a freezer bag for easier use).

HONEY DRESSING

- ⅓ cup sugar
- ¼ teaspoon dry mustard
- 1 teaspoon celery seed
- ½ teaspoon salt
- ½ teaspoon paprika
- 3 tablespoon honey, slightly warmed
- 3 tablespoons lemon juice
- ½ cup olive oil

Combine the sugar, mustard, celery seed, salt and paprika. Beat in the honey, lemon juice and oil. Mix thoroughly. Good over mixed greens or fruit salads. About 1 ¼ cups

HOT DOG CHILI

- 1 pound ground beef, cooked and drained
- 1 small onion, chopped
- 1 (6-ounce) can tomato paste
- 3 tomato paste cans of water
- ½ cup catsup
- 1 teaspoon vinegar
- 1 ½ teaspoons chili powder
- 1 teaspoon salt
- 1 teaspoon black pepper
- 1 teaspoon garlic salt

Cook ground beef and drain. Add other ingredients and cook until thickened and thoroughly blended. About 3 cups

HOT SAUCE
(FOR HOT BOLOGNA SANDWICHES)

- ½ cup flour
- 1 cup catsup
- 2 tablespoons prepared mustard
- ½ cup vinegar
- ½ cup lemon juice
- ½ teaspoon garlic salt
- ½ teaspoon onion salt
- 3 teaspoons brown sugar
- 3 teaspoons red pepper flakes
- 2 teaspoons chili powder
- ½ stick butter
- 1 quart water
- Tabasco sauce to taste

Mix all ingredients and simmer until well blended and thickened. Refrigerates well for several weeks. Makes about 1 quart

HOT WINE MAYONNAISE

- 1 tablespoon dried onion flakes
- ¼ cup dry white wine
- 2 tablespoons chopped fresh parsley
- 1 tablespoon lemon juice
- ¾ cup mayonnaise

Add onion flakes to wine and let stand about 10 minutes. Add remaining ingredients and heat, stirring constantly until well blended. Serve over cooked asparagus. About 1 cup

MOCK HOLLANDAISE SAUCE

- 1 egg yolk
- ¾ cup plain, low-fat yogurt
- 2 tablespoons lemon juice
- ¼ teaspoon salt
- ⅛ teaspoon dry mustard

Beat egg yolk slightly in a heavy saucepan with ¼ cup yogurt, lemon juice, salt and mustard. Cook over low heat, stirring constantly until thick and smooth. Remove from heat. Slowly stir in remaining ½ cup yogurt; blend well. Serve warm over vegetables. May store in refrigerator for short period. 8 (1 ½ tablespoons) servings

OLIVE OIL SAUCES FOR PASTA

AGLIO OLIO:
In skillet heat 6 tablespoons olive oil over medium heat. Add 1 tablespoon minced garlic and ¼ teaspoon red pepper flakes; sauté 2 minutes. Toss with ¼ cup fresh chopped parsley and hot pasta. Season to taste

WILD MUSHROOM:
In skillet heat 3 tablespoons olive oil over medium heat. Add 1 tablespoon minced garlic and sauté 2 minutes. Add 4 ounces Shiitake and cultivated mushrooms, sliced; sauté 5 minutes. Stir in 5 tablespoons olive oil and 1 tablespoon soy sauce. Toss with ¼ cup fresh chopped parsley and hot pasta. Season to taste.

BROCCOLI AND CHEESE:
In skillet heat ¼ cup olive oil over medium heat. Add 2 teaspoons minced garlic; sauté 2 minutes. Add 4 cups broccoli florets and ¾ cup chicken broth; cover and cook until broccoli is tender-crisp (about 3 minutes). Toss with ½ cup freshly grated Parmesan cheese and hot pasta. Season to taste.

PESTO I

- 1 cup packed fresh basil leaves
- 3 tablespoons pine nuts or chopped walnut, toasted and lightly cooled
- 1 large clove garlic
- 3 tablespoons freshly grated Parmesan cheese
- ⅓ cup olive oil

In a blender or small food processor blend together all ingredients with salt and pepper to taste until smooth. Can keep covered in the refrigerator up to one week. Makes about ⅔ cup.

PESTO II

- 4 cups loosely packed fresh basil leaves
- 1 cup freshly grated Parmesan cheese
- ½ cup pine nuts
- 1 ½ cups olive oil
- 3 cloves garlic
- ¼ teaspoon pepper.

Process all ingredients in an electric blender or food processor until smooth. Makes about 2 cups. To freeze: Put 2 tablespoons portions in each ice cube tray section. Freeze until firm, and then transfer to a large zip-lock freezer bag. Allow 1 cube per 2 ounces of pasta.

STIR FRY SAUCE MIX

- ½ cup cornstarch
- ¼ cup firmly packed brown sugar
- 1 tablespoon minced fresh ginger root
- 2 large cloves garlic, minced
- ½ teaspoon ground red pepper
- ½ cup soy sauce
- ¼ cup cider vinegar
- 2 cups chicken or beef broth
- ½ cup dry sherry
- ⅓ cup water

In a 1-quart jar combine first 5 ingredients. Add soy sauce and vinegar; shake until blended. Add broth, sherry and water; shake well. Store covered in refrigerator up to 2 weeks; shake before using. Mix may be frozen in tightly covered containers in 1-cup (usually enough for 4 servings) portions; thaw and shake before using. Makes 4 cups

DESSERTS

APPLE BROWN BETTY

Crumb mixture:
- 1 ½ cups fresh breadcrumbs
  (from about 3 slices white or whole-wheat bread)
- ¾ cup brown sugar, well packed
- 1 teaspoon freshly grated orange peel (optional)
- ½ teaspoon ground cinnamon
- 6 medium-size Granny Smith apples peeled, cored,
  quartered and thinly sliced (8 cups)
- 4 tablespoons butter cut into small pieces
- ¼ cup water

Pre-heat oven to 375 degrees. Mix crumb mixture and set aside. Arrange half the apple slices over the bottom of an un-greased 1 ½ quart baking dish. Sprinkle with half of the crumb mixture and dot with half the butter. Repeat with remaining apples, crumb mixture and butter. Drizzle with the water. Cover and bake about 45-55 minutes or until apples in the center are tender. Serve warm or at room temperature. 6 servings

APPLE TUBE CAKE

- 2 cups sugar
- 1 cup vegetable oil
- 3 eggs
- 2 ¼ cups all purpose flour, sifted
- 1 ½ teaspoon baking soda
- ½ teaspoon salt
- 1 teaspoon cinnamon
- 1 teaspoon allspice
- 1 teaspoon nutmeg
- 1 ½ cups peeled, chopped apples
- 1 cup buttermilk
- 1 cup chopped walnuts
- 1 teaspoon vanilla

Pre-heat oven to 350 degrees. Beat first 3 ingredients with electric mixer for 5 minutes. Add flour, soda, salt, spices, vanilla, buttermilk and mix, Then add apples, nuts and mix by hand. Bake in a tube pan for 60-70 minutes or until knife inserted comes out clean. While cake is baking make following glaze and pour over while cake still warm. Then let cool in pan before removing.

Orange Glaze:
- ¼ cup orange juice
- 2 tablespoons melted butter
- ½ pound powdered sugar

Mix well and pour over cake. 6 servings

APPLESAUCE CRISPY

- 1 cup biscuit mix
- ½ cup sugar
- ¼ cup butter
- 16 ounces applesauce
- ½ cup raisins
- ½ cup light brown sugar
- ½ cup chopped walnuts
- ½ teaspoon cinnamon
- ¼ teaspoon nutmeg

Preheat oven to 400 degrees. Combine biscuit mix and white sugar and set aside. Cut in butter until mixture crumbly. Combine remaining ingredients and pour into a 9-inch pie pan or an 8-inch baking dish. Sprinkle top with biscuit mix. Bake for about 20 minutes and serve hot. 6 serving

BENNE SEED COOKIES

- ¾ cup (1 ½ sticks) butter
- 1 ½ cups light brown sugar (firmly packed)
- 2 eggs
- 1 ¼ cups all-purpose flour
- ½ cup toasted benne seeds*
- 1 teaspoon vanilla extract
- ¼ teaspoon baking powder

*Pre-heat oven to 350 degrees. Place benne seeds in a shallow baking pan and bake for 10-15 minutes, stirring occasionally for uniform color. Bake until GOLDEN, NOT BROWN. Stir before using.

Preheat oven to 325 degrees. Cream butter and sugar together and mix with other ingredients in order. Line an un-oiled cookie sheets with waxed paper. Drop dough by the teaspoon on waxed paper about 2-inches apart Bake 10-20 minutes (watch carefully as these cookies burn easily). Cool on waxed paper, then peel off. Makes 3 dozen.

CARAMEL PUMPKIN FLAN

- ⅔ cup sugar
- 1 (12-ounce) can evaporated milk
- 2 (3-inch) cinnamon sticks
- 1 cup canned pumpkin
- 3 large eggs
- ¼ cup light brown sugar (packed firmly)
- 2 teaspoons vanilla extract
- ¼ teaspoon salt

Pre-heat oven to 350 degrees. Lightly oil a fluted 8 x 2-inch metal mold or flan dish. In a large, heavy skillet melt sugar over low heat without stirring until golden brown. Do not stir as sugar melts but swirl skillet to facilitate melting. Pour melted sugar (caramel) into the oiled mold, tilting to coat bottom; set aside.

In same skillet heat milk and cinnamon sticks over medium heat until bubbles appear around side of skillet, stir occasionally. Remove from heat and discard cinnamon sticks. With wire whisk combine pumpkin, eggs, brown sugar, vanilla and salt and mix until smooth. Beat in heated milk until well mixed and pour into mold. Place mold in a 13 x 9-inch baking pan with enough hot water to come up halfway on mold. Bake flan 65-75 minutes or until knife inserted in the center comes out clean.

Remove from oven and cool on rack to room temperature. Refrigerate flan at least 3 hours before serving. To serve, loosen flan around the edge with a small spatula. Place inverted plate on top. Holding plate and flan mold, invert to un-mold the flan. 8 servings

CARROT CAKE

- 4 eggs
- 2 cups sugar
- 2 cups self-rising flour
- 1 teaspoon cinnamon
- 1 cup vegetable oil
- 4-5 medium carrots ground of grated (I prefer grated)
- 1 cup chopped nuts (walnuts are good)
- 1 teaspoon vanilla

Pre-heat oven to 350 degrees. Beat eggs, add sugar and beat well. Sift flour, cinnamon and add alternately with oil. Add vanilla, carrots and nuts and blend well. Place in a greased and floured tube pan and bake for 1 ¼ hours or until knife inserted comes out clean.

Glaze:
- 1 cup sugar
- ½ cup buttermilk
- 1 teaspoon vanilla
- ½ teaspoon baking soda

Bring sugar and milk to boil and boil for one minute. Remove from heat, add vanilla and baking soda and mix well. Pour over cake while still warm. 8 servings

CHERRY COBBLER

- 40 ounces cherry pie filling
- 15 ounces of dark canned cherries
- ¼ cup all-purpose flour, divided
- ½ teaspoon almond extract
- 5 slices white bread
- 1 ¼ cups sugar
- ½ cup butter, melted
- 1 large egg
- 1 ½ teaspoons grated lemon rind

Pre-heat oven to 350 degrees. Stir together pie filling, cherries and 2 tablespoons flour. Stir in almond extract. Place in a lightly greased 8-inch square baking dish. Trim crusts from bread and cut slices into strips, Arrange strips over fruit mixture in pattern or choice. Stir together remaining 2 tablespoons flour, sugar, butter, egg and lemon rind. Drizzle over the bread strips. Bake for 35-40 minutes. 8-10 servings

CHOCOLATE ECLAIR CAKE

- 2 packages instant French vanilla pudding
- 2 ½ cups milk
- 8 ounces of Cool Whip
- 1 box graham crackers

Topping:
- ⅓ cup cocoa
- ¼ stick butter
- ¼ cup milk
- 1 teaspoon vanilla
- 1 cup confectioners sugar

Mix pudding and milk together. Add Cool Whip and mix until thickened. Lightly grease a 9 x 13-inch oblong pan and line with graham crackers. Pour half of the pudding mixture over graham crackers. Add another layer of graham crackers and pour remaining pudding mixture over them. Add a third layer of graham crackers. Mix cocoa, sugar and milk. Cook until boiling, stirring constantly so it won't stick. Cook 2 minutes. Remove from heat and add ¼ stick butter and 1 teaspoon vanilla (if butter doesn't melt hold over warm burner and stir well). Mix and let cool. Spread over the last layer of graham crackers. Refrigerate until ready to serve (at least one hour but better overnight). 12 servings

CINNAMON PIE

- 1 prepared piecrust, unbaked
- 2 eggs, slightly beaten
- 3 tablespoons flour
- ½ cup sugar
- 1 ½ cups milk or light cream
- 2 teaspoons ground cinnamon

Pre-heat oven to 325 degrees. Beat all ingredients together and pour into the unbaked piecrust. Bake for 25-30 minutes or until set. 6-8 servings

FLAN

- 1 cup sugar
- 4 eggs, beaten
- 14 ounces of sweetened condensed milk
- 1 ¾ cups milk
- 2 teaspoons vanilla
- ½ cup sliced almonds, toasted

Pre-heat oven to 350 degrees. Pour sugar into a 10-inch cast iron skillet on medium heat. Stir constantly with a wooden spoon until sugar melts and becomes light golden brown. Pour syrup into a 9-inch round cake pan and set aside. Combine eggs and next 3 ingredients and beat well using a wire whisk. Pour over the caramelized sugar, cover with aluminum foil and place in a large shallow pan. Pour hot water to depth of 1-inch in larger pan. Bake for 55 minutes or until knife inserted near center comes out clean. Remove pan from water and uncover, let cool on a wire rack. Cover and chill 4-6 hours. Loosen edges with a spatula. Invert flan onto a plate; arrange almonds around the edge. 8 servings

EASY FRUIT COBBLER

- 1 cup self-rising flour
- 1 cup milk
- 3 ½ to 4 cups chopped or sliced fruit
- ¼ cup sugar
- 1 stick butter
- 1 cup sugar

Pre-heat oven to 350 degrees. Mix flour, milk and ¼ cup sugar together for the batter. Melt butter in a 9 ½ x 13-inch pan. When butter is melted, pour batter on top. Put fruit on top of the batter and sprinkle 1 cup sugar over all. Bake for 40 minutes. 6-8 servings

FRESH PEACH PIE

- 1 uncooked prepared pie shell
- Fresh sliced peaches
- 1 cup sugar
- 1 tablespoon flour
- ⅔ cup half-and-half

Pre-heat oven to 350 degrees. Line pie shell with sliced fresh peaches. Mix together the sugar and flour and sprinkle over the peaches. Pour the ⅔ cup half-and-half over the pie. Bake for one hour. 6 servings

HAWAIIAN WEDDING CAKE

- 2 eggs
- 2 cups all-purpose flour
- 1 ½ cups sugar
- 2 teaspoons baking soda
- 1 (20-ounce) can crushed pineapple with juice
- 1 cup chopped nuts

Frosting:
- 1 (8-ounce) package of cream cheese (softened)
- 1 teaspoon vanilla
- 1 ½ cups confectioner's sugar
- ¼ cup butter (softened)

Pre-heat oven to 350 degrees. Mix all cake ingredients with a spoon. Pour into a 9 x 13-inch greased, floured cake pan. Bake for 40-45 minutes (check after 35 minutes). Cool. Mix ingredients for frosting. Frost cooled cake and refrigerate until time to serve. 6-8 servings

IMPOSSIBLE PUMPKIN PIE

- ¾ cup sugar
- ½ cup Bisquick
- 2 tablespoons butter
- 1 (12-ounce) can evaporated milk
- 2 eggs
- 1 (16-ounce) can pumpkin
- 2 ½ teaspoons vanilla

Pre-heat oven to 350 degrees. Grease a 9-inch pie pan. Beat all ingredients until smooth (about one minute in a blender, two minutes with a hand mixer). Pour into pie pan. Bake about 50-55 minutes (or until knife in center comes out clean). 8 slices

INDIAN PUDDING

- 1 pint milk
- ¼ cup corn meal
- ⅓ cup dark molasses
- 1 egg, well beaten
- ⅛ teaspoon salt
- ¼ teaspoon cinnamon
- 1 tablespoon butter
- ¼ cup raisins

Pre-heat oven to 350 degrees. Combine butter, milk and salt, then scald. Slowly stir in cornmeal and cook in double boiler for about 20 minutes until thickened. Add egg, molasses, cinnamon and raisins. Bake in a buttered baking dish for about 2 hours. May be served hot or cold, plain, or with cream or vanilla ice cream. 4-6 servings

MARY JOE'S BUTTERHORNS

Pastry:
- 1 cup butter
- 2 cups all-purpose flour
- 1 egg yolk, beaten (save white)
- ½ cup sour cream

Filling:
- ¾ cup sugar
- 1 teaspoon cinnamon
- ¾ cup minced nuts

Pre-heat oven to 350 degrees. Cut butter into flour until it resembles crumbs. Combine egg yolk and sour cream. Blend into flour mixture. Chill pastry overnight in refrigerator or in freezer for several hours. Divide dough into 4 parts on lightly floured board. Roll each part into a 10-inch circle. Sprinkle ¼ of filling over each circle and cut into 12-16 wedges. Roll up from wide end and place on a lightly greased cookie sheet. Brush tops with egg white. Bake for 20 minutes or until lightly browned. 4 dozen

MARY LEE'S "SOUPED UP" GRAHAMS

- 1 box graham crackers or cinnamon graham crackers
- crushed pecans (cup plus)

Syrup:
- 2 sticks of butter
- 1 cup packed brown sugar

Pre-heat oven to 350 degrees. Heat butter and mix in sugar, stirring until mixture becomes syrupy. Grease a cookie sheet and place graham crackers on it. Spread tops with syrup using a vegetable brush. Top with nuts and bake about. 10 minutes.

MINI CHEESECAKES

- 12 vanilla wafers
- 16 ounces cream cheese, softened
- ½ cup sugar
- 1 teaspoon vanilla
- 2 eggs

Pre-heat oven to 325 degrees. Line muffin tin with foil liners. Place one vanilla wafer in each liner. Mix cream cheese, vanilla and sugar on medium speed until well blended. Add eggs. Mix well. Pour over wafers, filling each ¾ full. Bake for 25 minutes. Remove from pan when cool. Chill. Top with fruit, preserves, nuts or chocolate. 12 servings

OATMEAL CAKE

- 1 ¼ cups boiling water
- 1 cup regular oats
- ½ cup butter, softened
- 1 cup white sugar
- 1 cup brown sugar
- 1 teaspoon vanilla
- 2 eggs
- 1 ½ cups all purpose flour
- 1 teaspoon baking soda
- ½ teaspoon salt
- ¾ teaspoon cinnamon

Pre-heat oven to 350 degrees. In a large bowl pour boiling water over oats and let set for 20 minutes. Mix in all the rest of the ingredients. Bake for 50-55 minutes or until knife inserted comes out clean. Make icing while cake bakes.

Icing:
- ¼ cup melted butter
- ½ cup brown sugar
- 3 tablespoon condensed milk or half-and-half
- ⅓ cup chopped nuts
- ¾ cup shredded coconut

Combine all ingredients and spread over cooled cake. 10 servings

ORANGE-CRANBERRY CAKE

- 2 ½ cups all purpose flour, sifted
- 1 cup sugar
- 1 teaspoon baking powder
- 1 teaspoon baking soda
- ¼ teaspoon salt
- 1 cup fresh cranberries
- 1 cup chopped pecans
- 1 cup chopped dates
- 2 tablespoons grated orange rind
- 2 eggs, beaten
- 1 cup buttermilk
- ⅔ cup vegetable oil

Glaze:
- ⅓ cup orange juice
- ⅓ cup sifted powdered sugar

Pre-heat oven to 350 degrees. Grease and flour a 10-inch Bundt pan. Combine first five ingredients in mixing bowl. Add the next four ingredients and stir well. Combine the eggs, buttermilk and vegetable oil. Add to the flour mixture. Stir until thoroughly blended. Pour into Bundt pan. Bake for 50 minutes or until toothpick comes out clean. Cool in the pan for 10 minutes. Invert onto a large plate. Punch holes in the top of the warm cake and spoon over the warm glaze.

Glaze: Combine and heat until hot, but not boiling. 10 servings

PUDDING CREAM PIE

- 1 graham cracker crust prepared
- 8 ounces cream cheese
- 2 cups whole milk
- 1 package lemon instant pudding
- Graham cracker crumbs (optional)

Soften cream cheese and blend with ½ cup milk. Add remaining milk and pudding mix. Beat slowly. Pour into graham cracker crust. Sprinkle graham cracker crumbs over the top. Refrigerate for one hour before serving. 8 servings

PUMPKIN PUDDING

- 1 package (4-serving size) vanilla instant pudding and pie filling
- 1 ½ cups milk
- 1 cup heavy whipping cream
- 1 teaspoon pumpkin pie spice
- 1 cup canned pumpkin

Mix pudding, milk, ½-cup cream and pumpkin pie spice and beat with electric mixer until thickened. Stir in pumpkin and mix well. Place in four dessert bowls. Whip remaining cream and garnish each dessert with cream and added sprinkle of pumpkin spice. Chill until serving. 4 servings

RAISIN DATE BARS

Filling:
- 1 ½ cups raisins
- 1 ½ cups cut-up dates
- ¼ cup sugar
- 1 ½ cups water
- ½ cup chopped nuts

Bring first four ingredients to boiling over low heat, stirring occasionally. Continue boiling, stirring occasionally, until mixture thickens (about 10 minutes). Stir in nuts.

Batter:
- ½ cup butter, softened
- ¼ cup shortening
- 1 cup packed brown sugar
- 1 ½ cups all-purpose flour
- 1 teaspoon salt
- ½ teaspoon baking soda
- 1 cup quick-cooking oats

Preheat oven to 400 degrees. Prepare filling. Mix butter, shortening and brown sugar. Stir in flour, salt, baking soda and oats. Press half the mixture in a greased 13 x 9 x 2-inch rectangular pan. Spread filling over top; sprinkle with remaining mixture, pressing lightly. Bake about 25-30 minutes or until light brown. Cut while warm into bars. About 40 cookies

RUM CAKE

- 1 box yellow cake mix with pudding in the mix
- 4 eggs
- ½ cup salad oil
- ½ cup dark rum (80 proof)
- ½ cup chopped nuts

Preheat oven to 325 degrees. Grease and flour a 10-inch tube or 12-inch Bundt pan. Sprinkle the chopped nuts. Mix cake ingredients and pour batter over nuts. Bake for 1 hour. While cake is baking make the glaze. Remove the cake from the oven and prick top with toothpick. Pour glaze over the cake while it is in the pan. Cool and remove cake from pan.

Glaze:
- 1 stick of butter
- 1 cup sugar
- ½ cup water
- 1 ounce dark rum (80 proof)

Boil first 3 ingredients, stirring constantly for 1 minute. Remove from heat, add rum and mix well. 8 servings

SPICY PUMPKIN BARS

- 4 large eggs
- 1 ¾ cups sugar
- 1 cup vegetable oil
- 2 cups canned pumpkin
- 2 cups all-purpose flour
- 2 teaspoons baking powder
- 1 teaspoon salt
- 2 teaspoons pumpkin pie spice
- 1 cup golden or black raisins

Pre-heat oven to 350 degrees. Beat eggs with mixer until frothy; beat in sugar and beat for two minutes. Beat in oil and pumpkin. Sift dry ingredients over raisins and fold dry mixture into egg mixture. Do not over mix. Pour into a greased and floured 13 x 9-inch pan. Bake for 35-40 minutes until done. Cool on rack and cut into 24 squares. 24 servings

STRAWBERRY YOGURT PIE

- 2 containers (8-ounces each) strawberry yogurt *
- ½ cup crushed strawberries
- 1 container (8 or 9-ounces) non-dairy whipped topping, thawed
- 1 prepared graham cracker piecrust

Combine fruit and yogurt in a bowl. Fold in whipped topping, blending well. Spoon into the crust and freeze 4 hours. Remove from freezer and place in refrigerator 30 minutes (or longer for a softer texture) before serving. Store any leftover pie in the freezer. 8 servings

*or other fruits (with matching yogurt)

- ½ cup crushed raspberries or blueberries
- 1 (8-ounce) can sliced peaches or apricot halves, drained and mashed
- 1 (8-ounce) can crushed pineapple, drained

SWEET POTATO PIE

- 1 prepared piecrust baked according to directions
- ½ cup brown sugar
- 2 teaspoons flour
- ⅓ teaspoon salt
- ¾ teaspoon cinnamon
- ¾ teaspoon ginger
- 1 cup cooked, mashed sweet potatoes
- 1 cup evaporated milk
- 1 ½ teaspoon molasses

Pre-heat oven to 350 degrees. Mix all ingredients well. Place in prepared piecrust and bake for 30-40 minutes until filling set. 8 servings

TART (QUICHE) PASTRY

- 2 cups sifted all-purpose flour
- 5 ounces chilled unsalted butter
- ¼ to ½ teaspoon salt
- 1 egg yolk with enough ice water to make ⅓ cup

Mix flour and salt together in a bowl. Cut butter in small cubes and mix into flour until crumbly. Beat ice water and egg yolk together. Sprinkle over flour and mix quickly. Gather into a ball, wrap in plastic and chill for 30 minutes. Roll out, fit into pan or pans. Chill in refrigerator for 30 minutes before baking.

FOR SWEET TART PASTRY: Add 1 tablespoon sugar to recipe, mixed with flour and salt.

Enough pastry for one (9 or 10-inch) quiche or tart pan, or 6-8 individual tart pans. Any remaining dough may be wrapped tightly and stored in freezer.

INDEX

Bourbon:
Bourbon Glazed Ham 21
Bran Muffins 152
Sweet Potatoes with Pecans 139

Breads:
Betty O'Shea's Irish Soda Bread 152
Caraway/Raisin Soda Bread
    Rolls 153
Cheddar Apple Bread 153
Cheese Biscuits 154
Cheesy Zucchini and Onion
    Flatbreads 154
Cranberry Pumpkin Bread 155
Easy Cheese Biscuits 155
Oatmeal Banana Bread 156
Orange Bread 156
Pear Zucchini Bread 157
Quick Little Cheese Breads 158
Sweet Potato Muffins 158
Vegetable Pizza 150
Whole Wheat Bread
    (Billie Mae's) 159
Zucchini Bread 159

Broccoli:
Baked Broccoli 110
Broccoli and Celery Casserole 114
Broccoli-Blue Cheese Casserole 115
Broccoli and Cheese Olive Oil
    Sauce for Pasta 165
Broccoli-Parmesan Gratin 115
Broccoli Pasta and Pesto 20
Broccoli Raisin Salad 87
Broccoli-Rice Casserole 116
Broccoli Salad 87
Cheesy Vegetable Supreme 119
Chicken-Broccoli Casserole 23
Curried Broccoli Salad 90
Easy Cheesy Broccoli Soup 6
End of Summer Vegetable Bake 34
Jellied Broccoli Salad 95
Marinated Vegetables 128
Penne with Broccoli 50
Rigatoni with Chicken, Broccoli 54
Seafood Pasta Salad 102
Stir Fry Beef and Vegetables 72
Swiss Broccoli Casserole 139
Tuna Pasta Salad 106
Vegetable Pasta 82

Vegetable Pizza 150
Veggie Lasagne 83

Brussels Sprouts:
Brussells Sprouts and Rice 116

Cabbage:
Boiled One Pot Dinner 20
Coleslaw 89
Creamed Cabbage 122
Mrs. Howard's Baked Cabbage 131
Sausage and Cabbage 57
Sausage Bean Soup 11
Savory Stuffed Cabbage 58
Smothered Cabbage Wedges 136
Unstuffed Cabbage 81

Cakes:
Carrot Cake 172
Chocolate Éclair Cake 173
Hawaiian Wedding Cake 175
Mini Cheesecakes 178
Oatmeal Cake 178
Orange-Cranberry Cake 179
Rum Cake 181

Carrots:
Boiled One Pot Dinner 20
Carrot Cake 172
Cashew Rice Pilaf 117
Chicken Stir Fry 26
Chicken Vegetable Stir Fry 27
Coleslaw 89
Creamy Carrot Soup 5
Ginger Carrots 126
Golden Rice 126
Grilled Chicken and Pasta Salad 93
Honey Glazed Carrots 127
Landlubber's Chowder 9
Left Over Turkey (Chicken)
    Rice Soup 10
Macaroni and Veggie Salad 98
Marie's Mac Salad 99
Marinated Vegetables 128
Monastery-Style Lentils 130
Sausage Bean Soup 11
Stir Fry Chicken and Vegetables 72
Veggie Lasagne 83

185

ABOUT THE AUTHOR

Barbara Beury McCallum is proud to be a native West Virginian. Her great-grandfather, Col. Joseph Lawton Beury, came from Pennsylvania to Fayette County, WV in the 1870s and was a pioneer coal operator. A monument to his achievements is located at Quinnimont, WV. A liberal arts education at Sweet Briar College (Virginia) gave her the opportunity to pursue many interesting careers from travel writing and public relations to nursing home administration and social work. Her poetry and short stories have been published nationally. Two constants throughout her life, however, have been the love of good food, perhaps from her French heritage (traced to 1066) and of writing, possibly stemming from an active imagination that at a young age created her alter ego, Sophie.